The Well Dressed Child

Children's Clothing 1820-1940

Anna MacPhail

Schiffer Publishing Ltd

4880 Lower Valley Road, Atglen, PA 19310 USA

Dedication

To my darling Michael for all
his patience and encouragement.

MacPhail, Anna.
    The well dressed child/Anna MacPhail.
      p. cm
    Includes bibliographical references.
    ISBN 0-7643-0858-0 (hardcover)
    1. Children--Costume--Great Britain--History--
19th century. I. Title
GT737.M33   1999
391'.3'094109034--dc21   99-17204
                           CIP

Designed by "Sue"
Type set in ZapfChan Bd BT/Aldine 721 BT

ISBN: 0-7643-0858-0
Printed in China
1 2 3 4

Published by Schiffer Publishing Ltd.
4880 Lower Valley Road
Atglen, PA 19310
Phone: (610) 593-1777; Fax: (610) 593-2002
E-mail: Schifferbk@aol.com
Please visit our web site catalog at
www.schifferbooks.com

This book may be purchased from the publisher.
Include $3.95 for shipping.
Please try your bookstore first.
We are interested in hearing from authors
with book ideas on related subjects.
You may write for a free catalog.

In Europe, Schiffer books are distributed by
Bushwood Books
6 Marksbury Rd.
Kew Gardens
Surrey TW9 4JF England
Phone: 44 (0)181 392-8585; Fax: 44 (0)181 392-9876
E-mail: Bushwd@aol.com

Contents

Pricing

All the prices in this book are based on a
garment that is all original with no holes, stains,
or alterations and in fully restored condition.

Acknowledgments

To Linda Simone for her help, time, and friendship, which have been invaluable to me; Jackie Waigel of 'Badjiboodi' for allowing me to borrow some of her many beautiful dolls as props; Karen Tripp of 'Wings of Time' for her cooperation; and my son, Kyle Mac Phail, for his constructive advice.

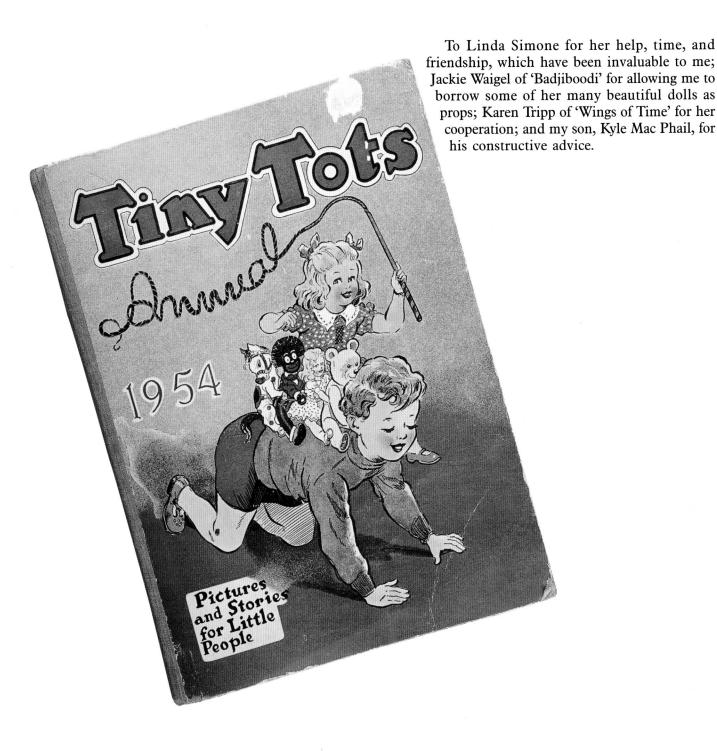

Introduction

My earliest recollection of being drawn to old things, especially fabrics, is when as a small girl I was taken to the 'Barrows' in Glasgow, Scotland, by my father. The 'Barrows' is a flea market that continues still to this day, every Friday, Saturday, and Sunday. Contrary to my two elder brothers, who were constantly bored and complaining of 'aching legs,' I was in seventh Heaven there, surrounded by stalls piled high with all kinds of old discarded materials and clothing. It was after the Second World War, and things were difficult in Britain, so my father was there for more practical reasons, looking for old tools to work with and scraps of leather and nails to mend our shoes. If I was extra-special good, to my delight, I would be allowed to choose a 'peg doll', a long wooden clothes peg, painted like a doll and dressed in colorful scraps of material. During their lifetimes, these 'peg dollies' would have many sets of clothing lovingly made by my small fingers.

Later, while at school in Glasgow, I was required to attend domestic science classes where young ladies were taught how to launder cloth in the proper manner. Meeting each Thursday, the class was made to take along a piece of linen (teacloth, pillowcase, petticoat, or a smallish article) and soak, boil, wash, starch, and iron it for three hours. How I dreaded Thursdays back then. Now these same tedious domestic science classes have stood me in good stead, as I have retained the knowledge of looking after and restoring all kinds of antique linens, clothing, and most fabrics.

I love all antique fashions, and enjoy restoring them back to their original state. I have an extra special penchant for children's clothing. There have been many good reference books written on fashion throughout the ages, but not so many on children's wear. This is one of the reasons I was prompted to write this book.

I am particularly interested in the Victorian Era of fashion which covers the main body of the book. Victoria, daughter of the Duke of Kent, was born in 1819, and she came to the throne as a young girl in 1837, when she was 18 years old. Despite her tender years, she had a strong personality, and she quickly restored the Monarchy's popularity at home and abroad. Her influence was so great and she also had a certain 'presence' about her, that her name is used to describe the greater part of the 19th century from 1837 to 1901 as the *Victorian Age*.

The best place to start of course is the beginning, so my first chapter begins with the birth and the layette.

The Well Dressed Child

The Victorian child had lots to wear
Today some of it is fine and rare
Dresses made of silk and fine cotton
With lacy frills to the yoke and bottom
Little boys too, wore velvet and frills
And often looked like little girls !
Tiny babies in long christening gowns
This one here, see how he frowns
Lovely bonnets framed small faces
With soft muslin and hand made laces
High button boots encased small feet
The Well Dressed Child is all complete

Chapter One

The Layette

In Victorian times, it was considered unlucky to have too many clothes put away for the expected child, as infant mortality was rife in all classes of society. Post natal infections and complications due to lack of hygiene and medical ignorance were often the cause. However, a certain amount of preparation for the birth of a new child was necessary. Childbirth was an important family event. It was also a heavy expenditure for working class families.

The abandonment of *swaddling clothes* took place in the 1800s. *Swaddling* refers to the wrapping of a baby in various lengths of fine materials instead of actual clothing.

Tiny muslin or linen first shirts were lovingly hand sewn, along with pure woolen wrap vests and fine linen binders to flatten the navel. These binders were wrapped firmly around the baby for the first eight weeks to ensure he or she would have a nice flat tummy button. Sometimes a copper penny would even be bound against the navel. It was essential to have at least two dozen fine woolen and cotton diapers and cambric petticoats for the baby. Heavier flannel petticoats were worn in colder weather. Finest *nunsveiling* or *vyella* materials, along with the softest Egyptian cotton, were used to make baby gowns. Matinee jackets, warm bootees, bonnets, and always a 'shawly' were also made. Baby shawls were knitted with the finest of Shetland wool in a gossamer spider's web design with points all around. When the shawl was completed, the floor rugs (there were no fitted carpets at that time) were lifted and the shawl was stretched out and pinned between sheets of paper to the floorboards. The rugs were then replaced and walked on for several weeks. The result was a perfectly pressed out shawl.

A baby was to be wrapped firmly for the first few weeks, as this was thought to guarantee nice straight limbs

Of course, in the early 1800s, there were no plastic pants, only woolen or cotton ones. So, when a baby was wet, he or she would have to be completely changed. Several sets of clothing were necessary and the well-to-do baby had an abundance of attire.

Little books were printed out to advise mothers-to-be what to have ready for the approaching birth. It was considered 'bad luck' to start these preparations too soon. Given the amount of work that went into the infant clothing, the sewing had to start reasonably early, so that there would be adequate supplies for the newborn.

The following photographs are examples of baby *Layettes* from around 1840 up until the 1950s, illustrating the variety of layettes made for babies.

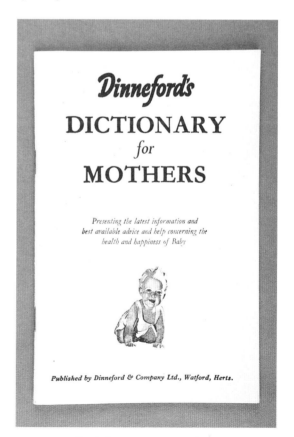

Book for expectant mothers.

Suggestions for Layette.

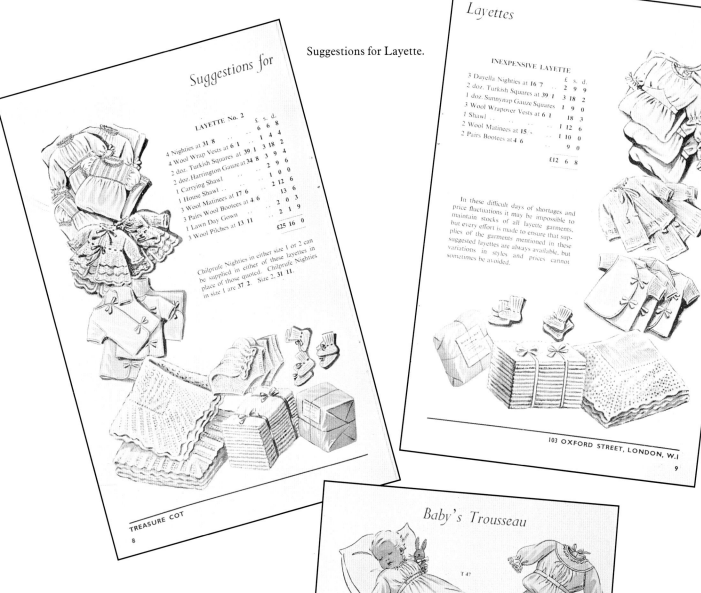

Suggestions for

LAYETTE No. 2

	£	s.	d.
		6	6	8
4 Nighties at 31 8			
4 Wool Wrap Vests at 6 1	1	4	4
2 doz. Turkish Squares at 39 1	3	18	2
2 doz. Harrington Gauze at 34 8	3	9	4
1 Carrying Shawl	2	9	6
1 House Shawl	1	0	0
3 Wool Matinees at 17 6	2	12	6
3 Pairs Wool Bootees at 4 6		13	6
1 Lawn Day Gown	2	0	3
3 Wool Pilches at 13 11	2	1	9
	£25	**16**	**0**

Chilprufe Nighties in either size 1 or 2 can be supplied in either of these layettes in place of those quoted. Chilprufe Nighties in size 1 are 37 2. Size 2, 31 11.

TREASURE COT

8

Layettes

INEXPENSIVE LAYETTE

	£	s.	d.
3 Dayella Nighties at 16/7	2	9	9
2 doz. Turkish Squares at 39 1	3	18	2
1 doz. Sunnynap Gauze Squares	1	9	0
3 Wool Wrapover Vests at 6 1		18	3
1 Shawl	1	12	6
2 Wool Matinees at 15/-	1	10	0
2 Pairs Bootees at 4 6		9	0
	£12	**6**	**8**

In these difficult days of shortages and price fluctuations it may be impossible to maintain stocks of all layette garments, but every effort is made to ensure that supplies of the garments mentioned in these suggested layettes are always available, but variations in styles and prices cannot sometimes be avoided.

103 OXFORD STREET, LONDON, W.1

9

More suggestions.

Baby's Trousseau

T 47

CHILPRUFE

T 47. Infant's Nightie of wool and cotton mixture with inset sleeve and lace trimmed neck and sleeves.

Price **31/8**

CHILPRUFE

Chilprufe Nightie (all wool) available in two sizes and made with round yoke and raglan sleeves giving ample growth allowances.

Size 1 37/2   Size 2 31/11

No. 1055. Shawls in silk and wool mixture.
Price from 32/6 to 49/6

L. 88. All wool Utility Shawls in various patterns.
Price from 31/6 to 37/6

SHETLAND

Real Shetland hand-knitted Shawls in various sizes.
Price from £4.0.0 to £5.5.0

No. 1055

L. 88

SHETLAND

TREASURE COT

4

8

Books for expectant mothers.

From milk
to mixed diet

A GUIDE TO MODERN BABY FEEDING

FAREX
GUIDE
TO
WEANING

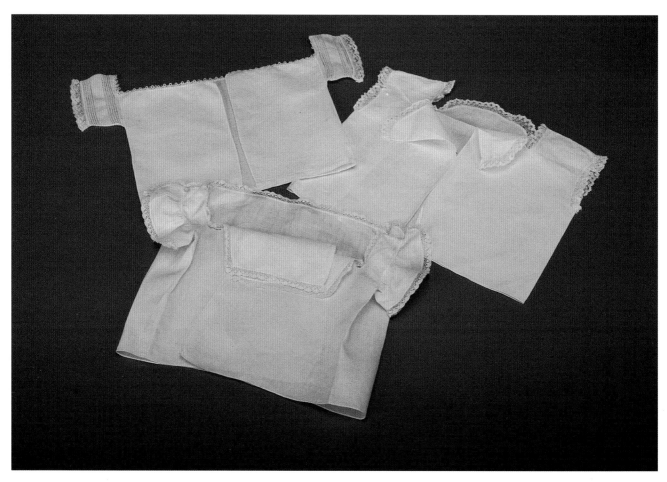

Tiny linen 'first' shirts worn next to the skin, in various styles, c.1860–1880.

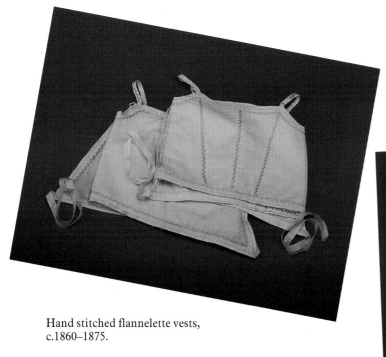

Pure wool and silk knitted vests and *vyella* jacket, c.1860–1880.

Hand stitched flannelette vests, c.1860–1875.

Crib sheet, brushed cotton blanket, and wool receiving blanket, c.1890-1920.

Flannelette wrap around petticoat, buttons on shoulder, c.1880.

Cotton diaper pants with button closures, c.1890.

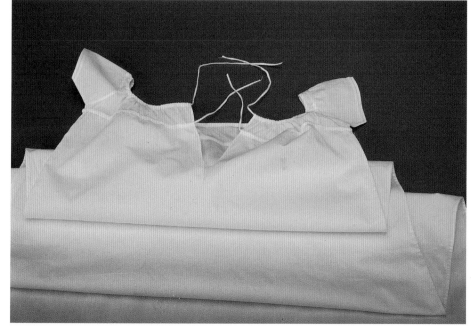

Early Victorian long cotton gown with wide neck and ties at back, c.1840.

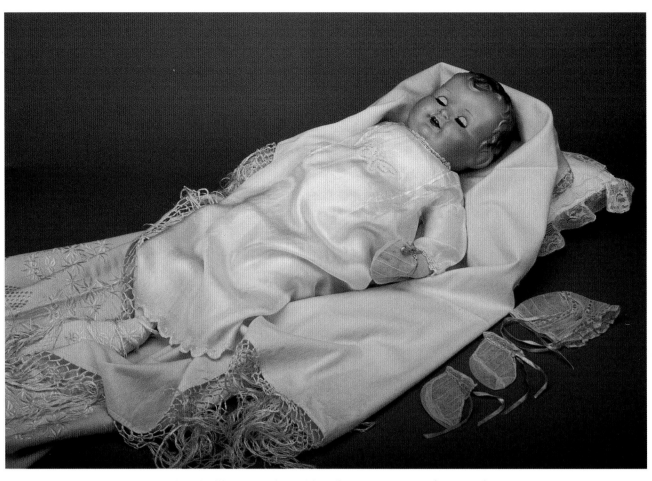

Hand made silk gown and matching slip. Note lace butterfly on the front together with lace mittens, bootees, and bonnet, c.1930. $125.

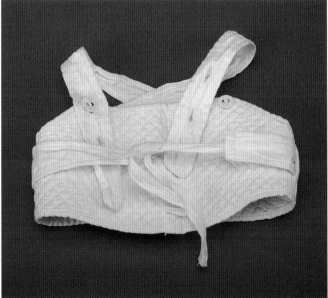

Quilted cotton binder, wraps and ties around with adjustable buttons on the shoulders, c.1870 . $50.

Heavy wool and cotton long petti-coat, c.1900. $30.

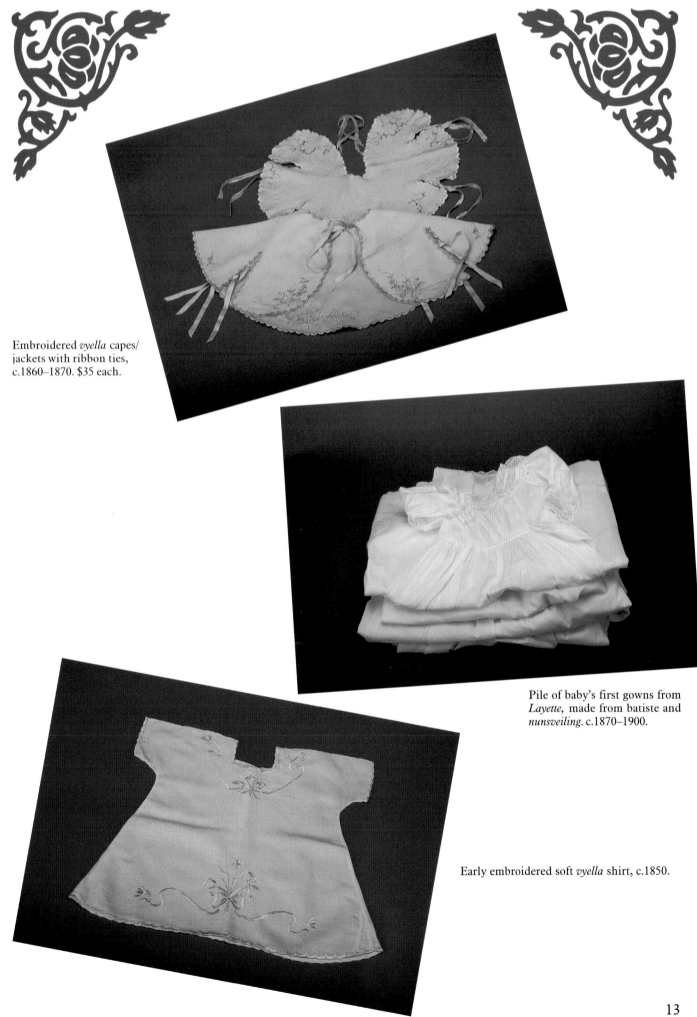

Embroidered *vyella* capes/
jackets with ribbon ties,
c.1860–1870. $35 each.

Pile of baby's first gowns from
Layette, made from batiste and
nunsveiling. c.1870–1900.

Early embroidered soft *vyella* shirt, c.1850.

Fine cotton matinee jacket, c.1900.

Cambric nightgown for boy or girl from Layette, c.1900. $85.

Knitted wool and silk jackets with silk ribbon ties, c.1860–1880. $50 each.

Hand made long cotton gown
from Layette, c.1873. $150.

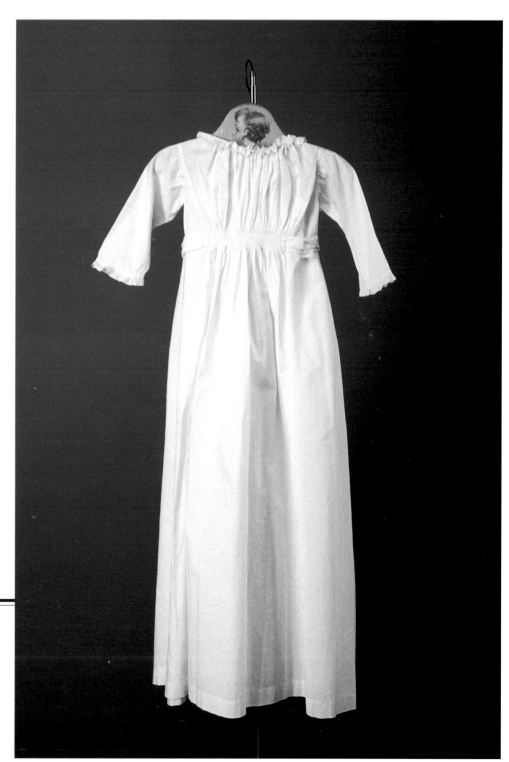

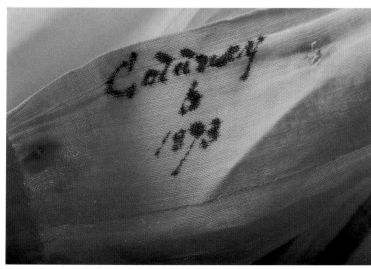

Date in the back of gown from c.1873.

Hand crocheted woolen jacket and shoulder cape with original silk ribbon ties, c.1870 . $65 each.

Hand knitted and crocheted bootees, c.1920 . $20 each set.

Hand crocheted woolen coat, c.1880. $60.

Linen chemise, c.1900.

Cradle Roll Card, 1911.

Cradle Roll Card, 1903.

A few days after the birth of the baby, the parents would usually enroll the child in the Church. They were then given a Cradle Roll card with the date of the enrollment.

Chapter Two

The Christening

In the 19th century, the Victorians were generally quite thrifty. In view of the fact that they had rather large families, when the christening gown was made for the first child, it was put together in a way that would allow for the garment to fit successive offspring whatever their size. Babies were mostly baptized at around six weeks old; unless they were delicate, then the formal christening would be postponed.

You will find most christening gowns have little drawstrings at the neck and waist. These strings could simply be let out for the chubbier baby or drawn tighter for the smaller sister or brother, allowing the gown to be handed down from generation to generation.

Around 1820, a popular magazine of the day, "*The Work Woman's Guide*," mentioned children's fashions for the first time, recommending the lengths of gowns for babies to be "at least 40 inches long for the wealthy, and 34 inches long for the poor."

Ayrshire work, sometimes called whitework, originated as far back as the 18th century in Europe from an embroidery called Dresden work. It was introduced into Scotland in 1814 by Mrs. Jamieson of Ayr, Scotland. She took advantage of the cotton mills which were situated in the moist climates of Edinburgh and Glasgow. The atmosphere in these two cities was ideal for cotton spinning. From here the industry grew. The mill owners organized people to work in groups in their own homes under a 'putter out.' Very fine work was produced by many ladies following the patterns of the manufacturers drawn up at the new Academies of Design in Glasgow and Edinburgh. Assembly type work was applied throughout the Ayrshire Industry; however, the standard and quality of the work was very high, and the finished gowns and bonnets were expensive to purchase. Pieces were often sold with the centers left blank to enable the purchaser to do the infills themselves with stitches of their choosing. It is very common to find gowns where the edgings do not match the embroidered panels, suggesting that they were finished separately.

The examples shown in this chapter are from around 1840 to 1900, and you will note how exquisite the work is. The items shown are much sought after and collected today.

Take notice of the front waistband on the Ayrshire work dresses from earlier in the last century. If the bodice is finished in a peak outside the band, then the dress was made for a boy. If the peak was sewn under the band and did not show, then it was traditionally made for a girl.

The beautiful gown and underslip in the first photo once belonged to the J & P Coats family (worldwide manufacturers and suppliers of sewing thread, from the 19th century to the present day). I was lucky enough to acquire these from a member of the family whom I met in the Orkney Islands in Scotland many years ago. The set was made by factory workers in the second half of the 19th century for the expected new baby. The petticoat is fine cotton lawn, with inserts of Torchon lace, and a scalloped deep frill. It is almost as ornate as the dress itself. The gown is 42 inches long and has wonderful little 'leg o' mutton sleeves, white hand embroidery lace flower inserts, and French knots, and is finished off with hand made Valenciennes lace.

Some of the dresses have short sleeves or no sleeves at all. When the weather was cool, the baby would be dressed in woolen vests with petticoats underneath, and then a christening cape over the top of the dress.

If a gown that had been handed down had short sleeves, and the next child in line was to be baptized in colder months, then it is not uncommon to find some gowns where long sleeves were added.

Opposite page:
Gown with J & P Coats provenance as described, together with underslip, 42" long, c.1885. $550.

Regarding the lace and frills that adorned the dresses and bonnets, it made no difference whether a child was male or female. Today when asking for a christening gown and bonnet, most parents do not want too many frills if it is for a boy!

Cream silk gowns were popular, but more delicate, so not as many survived. Some beautiful examples are shown here and all are in mint condition too. These should not be handled too much, as the acid in one's hands can cause them to deteriorate. These have all been stored in white *acid free* tissue, which helps to preserve all old silks and linens.

J & P Coats box.

Underslip for gown with J & P Coats provenance.

20

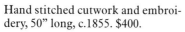

Hand stitched cutwork and embroidery, 50" long, c.1855. $400.

Ayrshire work gown for boy, 46" long, c.1870. The point of the yoke is over the waistband. $285.

Hand made Valenciennes lace inserts and whitework embroidery embellish this gown, 45" long, c.1865. $380.

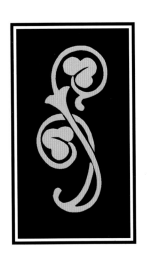

Gown with Ayrshire work, bottom put together with a different top, 45" long, c.1880. $195.

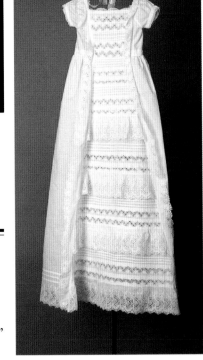

Gown with layered Broderie Anglaise frills down front, 42" long, c.1900. $265.

The gown on page 24 is a very early item from 1820 to 1830. Made of the finest muslin with exquisite embroidery, the gown is a fine example of early Ayrshire work. It must have taken an exceptionally long time to make. There are several darns on the dress and one has to study the dress closely to realize that these are there. The mends are interesting because they are wonderfully hand sewn on such sheer fabric, and are a work of art in themselves. This particular dress would require two petticoats underneath. I am sure a gown like this would have belonged to someone quite important and cost a good deal when it was commissioned to make.

Hand worked gown with cutwork all down the front, together with Mechlin lace inserts on the bodice, 46" long, c.1865. $365.

This gown is a beautiful example of early Ayrshire work executed on the finest of muslin. Drawstrings fasten the back. This material is so fine that it was worn with at least three underslips, 50" long, c.1840. $585.

Gown with cutwork embroidery and many pintucks, 45" long, c.1870. $225.

Close-up of gown on previous page showing a repair and how finely it has been sewn. The mend is probably about 90 years old.

Cream silk gown with inserts of machine Irish crochet lace, and edged with Mechlin lace, 42" long, c.1900. $165.

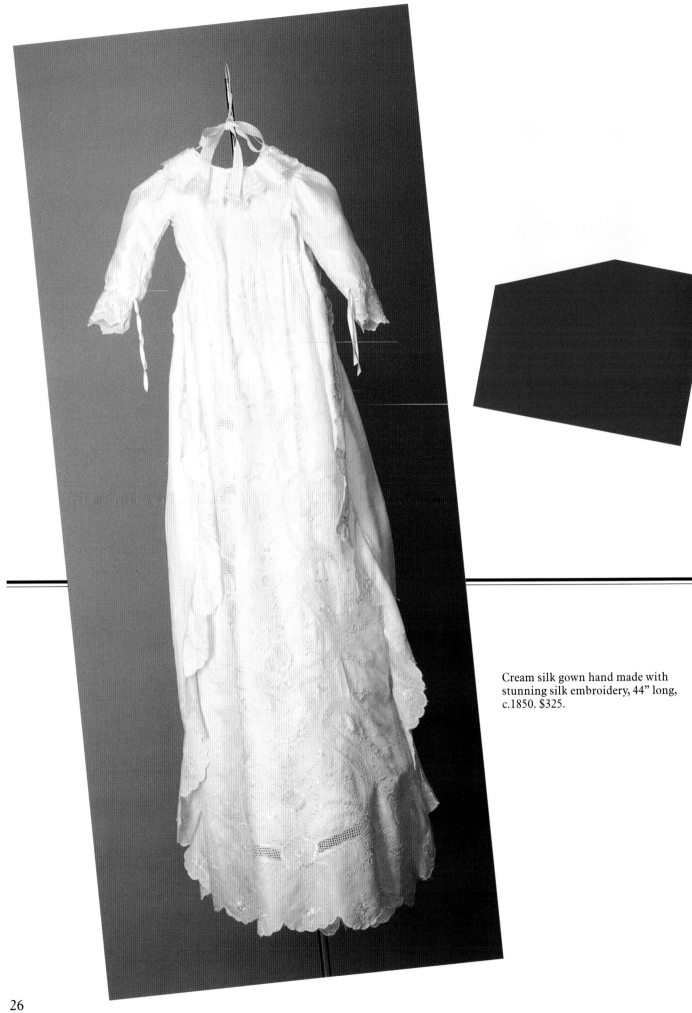

Cream silk gown hand made with stunning silk embroidery, 44" long, c.1850. $325.

Close-up of embroidery of cream silk gown.

Gown with Ayrshire work skirt, and added top of a different design, 44" long, c.1890. $185.

Opposite page:
Gown with Guipuire lace front panel,
41" long, c.1900. Very ornate. $350.

Gown with many hand bobbin lace
inserts, 38" long, c.1900. $350.

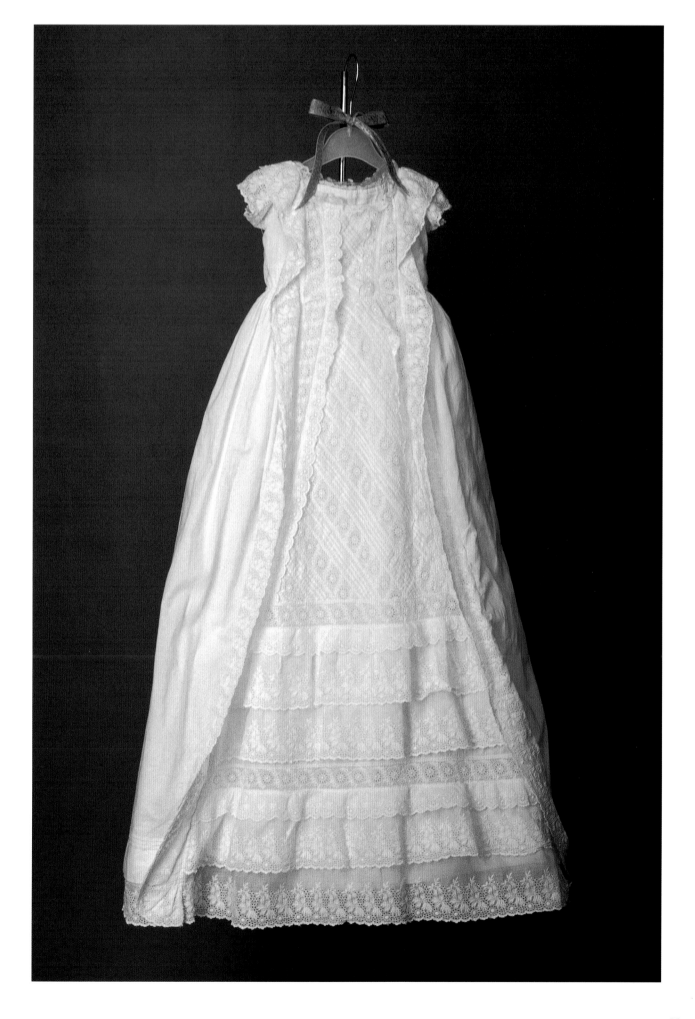

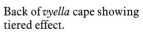

Vyella cape lined with silk, c.1860. Large cape collar. Heavily embroidered and trimmed in silk. Worn over long gowns. $225.

Back of *vyella* cape showing tiered effect.

Most dresses of this type were very long, the earlier the gown, the longer it was, and the more affluent the family. The gowns I have here measure from 35 inches long to 50 inches from shoulder to hem.

Many of these wonderful dresses can still be purchased today and are used for formal christenings. Many also appear in homes for adornment. Some are found hanging in guest bedrooms to be enjoyed by all. Others are used to dress baby sized bisque dolls. A few years ago I encountered a lady who told me she had a home in the mountains and, instead of curtains at her windows, she had hung many lovely baby gowns, as she loved them so much and wanted to see them in every room of the house.

Gown with whitework embroidery and long ties finishing in a large bow at the back, 44" long, c.1900. $185.

Detail of sleeve of gown with whitework embroidery. Note the tiny hand made buttons at cuff.

Christening coat in ribbed pique cotton, 37" long.

Gown with Broderie Anglaise lace embroidery to the yoke and around the bottom, 40" long, c.1910. $200.

Gown with machined eyelet decoration and ribbon threaded through waist, 42" long, c.1900. $185.

Christening coat as shown on
previous page with its very long cape
attatchment.

Ayrshire work gown for girl with the
point at waist sewn in, 42" long,
c.1890. $225.

Elaborate christening coat in ribbed cotton, heavily hand embroidered, 32" long.

Coat, similar to coat on previous
page, with its very long cape
attachment. Cape is 27" long, c.1900.
$300.

Studio photo of baby propped on a couch dressed in very long christening gown and petticoats, c.1890.

Silk christening gown hand made from parachute silk with simple lace trim and large sash, c.1943. Large size to fit 9 month old. $95.

Christening gown of heavy cotton
with pintucked and cutwork design
all the way down the front panel, 48"
long, c.1880. $275.

Fine almost sheer cape with stand
up collar and tiniest of button
closure at neck, c.1900. This
would have gone over a christening gown. $75.

Opposite page:
Displayed on a doll in a carriage, this splendid gown is hand made with layered frills worked with whitework embroidery in a finer cotton, 48" long, c.1875. $385.

Cream silk gown with overdress of net and lace, c.1950s. $50.

Heavy pique cape with Broderie trim for over christening coat or dress c.1920. $65.

A selection of four christening veils, from floral lace to plain fine net lace with ribbon trim, c.1890-1920. $50-75.

An example of a long petticoat worn under a gown, c.1870. $70.

An example of a long petticoat worn under a gown. Hand made with lace insertions and trim, c.1890. $65.

The drawstring ties at the back of some christening gowns and petticoats. See the small buttons.

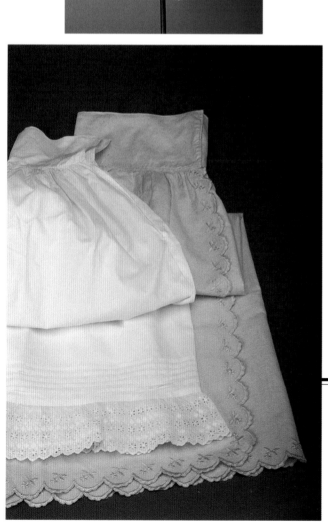

Two long petticoats, one flannelette and a fine cotton one worn over the top of the other, c.1880.

Lavish frills, whitework embroidery and lace adorn this full skirted christening gown and matching bonnet, 50" long, c.1870. Dress: $400.

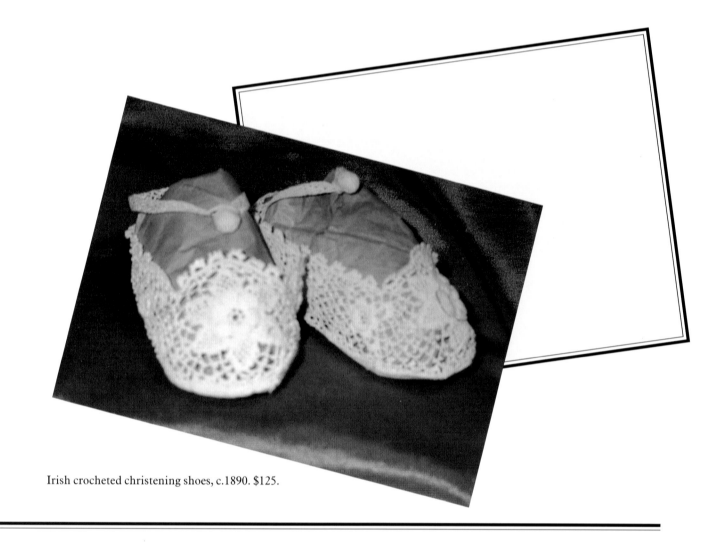

Irish crocheted christening shoes, c.1890. $125.

A lace making machine was introduced and patented by John Hatchcoat as early as 1808, and darned machine net was born. This machine-made lace fabric was a novelty and the crowns of baby caps began to be made of it and embroidered with tiny flowers. The fabric was similar in design and technique to Ayrshire work, but the good quality embroidered flowers had darned net fillings.

All of the gowns featured here would have taken a very long time to make, worked on day and night. Notice the amount of fine handwork executed. They would mostly have been made for privileged families who were of some importance or well to do, allowing them to afford the high costs.

The cream silk or woolen capes shown are christening capes to go over either the cotton gowns or silk ones. The capes were usually removed in the church or for photographs to show the gown underneath. Usually, they are found with beautiful embroidery and some also have lace trimmings. However, it is not too often one sees these intact, without damage to the silk or lining.

Now we come to the bonnets. Each one would have taken considerable time to make as they were mostly all hand sewn. Some have several frills around the face that when stretched out make for a long piece of material to hand stitch. Almost all bonnets are found edged with hand made Mechlin or Valenciennes lace. The same technique applies to the Ayrshire or whitework bonnets as with the gowns. (See Chapter six, "Bibs & Bonnets," for more information)

I have shown a bonnet from the early 1800s which is very rare today for its very fine example of Holliepoint lace. This is extremely fine work and, if you look very closely at the back panel, you will invariably see some kind of little animal, usually "the Lamb of God," in keeping with their purpose as christening bonnets. This particular one has a squirrel and underneath a small bird, which are nonetheless God's creatures. This lace was painstaking work and, as you may have realized, took an enormous amount of time to do. Many collector's only dream of finding Holliepoint lace.

Christening veils were made of very fine soft lace. The ground was usually plain with some decoration around the edges. They were placed over the baby's face upon entering the church, and removed to have the sign of the cross made on the baby's forehead.

The saddest little gown and hat here is the black one. These are extremely rare and very collectible. They were made for a child who was to be christened, but whose mother had died in childbirth. If a black dress could not be made or found in time for the christening, a black band was sewn around the sleeve of a white christening gown or sometimes a black silk sash was tied diagonally around the gown.

Rare black mourning christening gown, c.1870. Quilted silk with gold lace around neck, wide sleeves with hooks, and eyes at back.

There is a well-known picture that hangs in various National Trust houses that exemplifies the mourning style of dress for christening gowns. It features Queen Victoria in mourning for her grandmother, the Duchess of Kent, in 1860. She is shown with her son, Prince Wilhelm, who, just 3 years old, wears a black suit and the baby in her arms has a black crepe sash around the gown.

Chapter Three

Baby Girls & Boys

Basically, in the 19th century and up until around 1920, baby girls and boys were dressed much alike. They both wore white cotton, linen, or cream silk dresses. Jackets and skirts were also worn by both boys and girls.

Simple white batiste or cotton cambric gowns were worn on warm evenings without petticoats as night clothes. Most had little drawstring ties at the neck and waist. Some had the tiniest of buttons at the back so as not to press into the baby's back when laid down. Others were open down the back. Warm flannelette or vyella gowns were worn during the colder months with much the same design.

During the day, long white gowns were worn with one or two petticoats. These were quite a bit more decorative, adorned with hand embroidery or lace trims. Today, many people call any long gown a christening gown, and indeed the simpler long ones may be used for that now. However, most long gowns were for the most part everyday wear. Matinee jackets were worn over dresses. These could be frilly and fancy or quite plain and made of wool for added warmth.

Silk hand made dress to fit 6–9 month old, c.1920. $95.

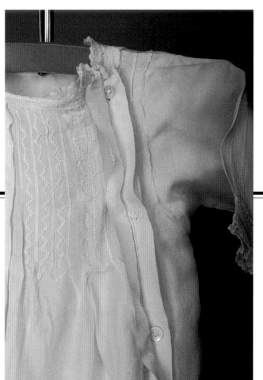

Close-up of silk dress showing tiny concealed buttons that fasten all the way up left side of front.

Cotton baby gown with Broderie Anglaise lace and pintucks down front to fit 9–12 month old, c.1920. $95.

Baby gown with hand made Mechlin lace inserts and trim around the bottom, 28" long, c.1890. Fastens with 3 tiny mother-of-pearl buttons at the back and has original narrow peach silk ribbon inserts. $285.

WALSH, MT. CARMEL, PA.

Charming photo of a little girl
holding a baby of around 9 months
old dressed in a white frilled day
gown, c.1890.

Baby gown of ribbed cotton pique with frilled yoke, c.1880. Long sleeves and 4 small buttons down back. $195.

Fine *nunsveiling* baby dress for 18-
month-old baby with delicate
embroidery, c.1910. $125.

Day gown made of plain lightweight
cotton, c.1890. Very simple with lace
trim and wide ties to back. $75.

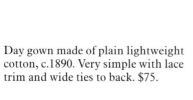

Photo of child in 1900 dressed in frilly cotton dress and petticoat.

Baby gown hand embroidered with shoulder pleats, c.1910. $165.

Baby boy's nightgown, simple but wonderfully hand sewn, c.1863. $175.

Detail showing the date found on the back of the gown underneath the buttoned belt. "Theobald" June 1863.

Voille machine embroidered gown for
baby boy, c.1920. $165.

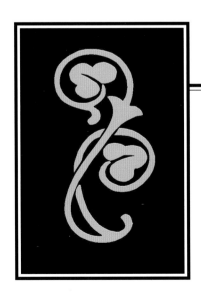

Crisp cotton day gown decorated
with drawn thread work, c.1880.
$175.

Baby dress with waistline and long
sleeves, c.1925. Machine made. $95.

Baby boy's lightweight cotton coat
with very large cape collar and
some hand embroidery and
mother-of-pearl buttons,
c.1910. $175.

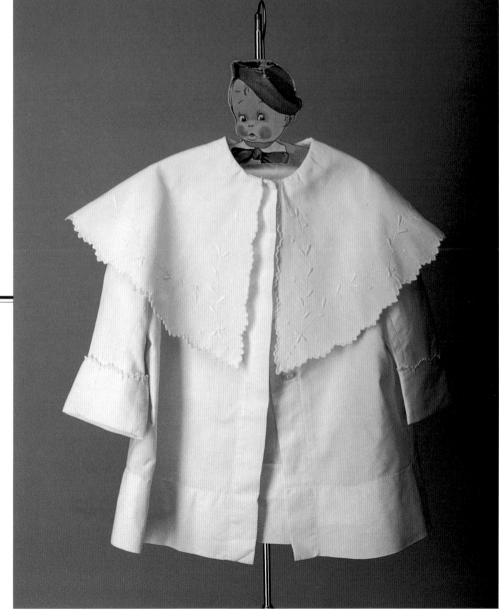

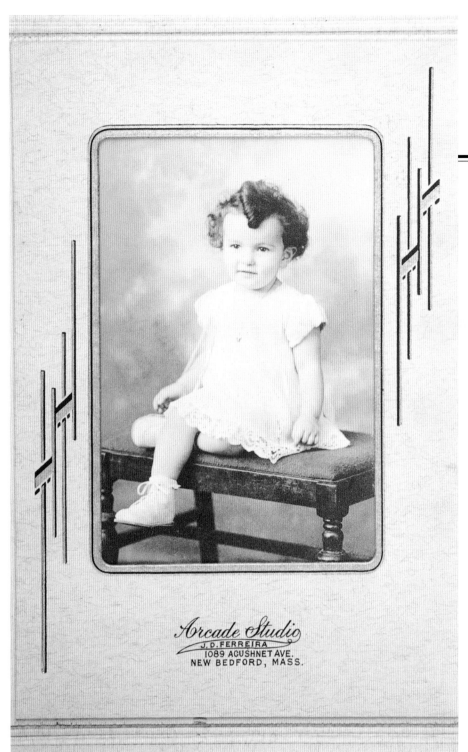

Photo taken in 1930 of a baby girl dressed
in a white cotton dress and little kid
leather lace up boots.

Very feminine baby gown with
puffed long sleeves and
Valenciennes lace yoke, c.1880.
$195.

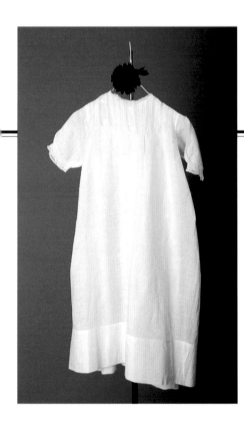

Everyday baby dress to fit 6–9 month old, soft white cotton with tiny hand embroidery, c.1920. $85.

Everyday dress for baby 6–9 months old, pretty embroidered yoke with many pintucks, c.1920. $85.

Fine lawn baby gown for 9 month old, delicately hand embroidered with label inside the neck edge indicating "strictly hand made," c.1930. $85.

Silk baby gown with smocking to the front yoke and concealed buttons down the left side of the front, c.1900. $125.

Pretty silk matinee jacket edged with layers of lace and 3 tiny buttons to close, c.1880. $85.

Silk baby gown and jacket, c.1920. The dress is hand smocked at the yoke and has double frills at the bottom. The jacket has never been worn and is edged with blue silk. The blue silk ribbon ties are original. $200.

Silk coat with large attached cape and collar, c.1900. Delicate hand lace trim and silk ribbon belie the practicality of the coat's warm flannel lining. $195.

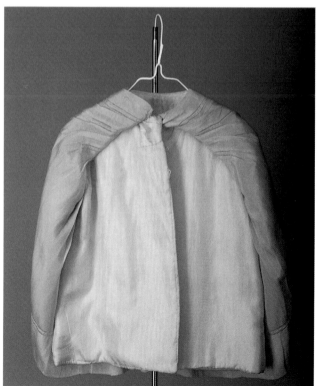

Warm flannel lining

Fine quality jacket for 4–6 month old,
c.1890. Linen with whitework embroidery
and hand bobbin lace. $135.

Child's wonderful high quality fine cotton coat to fit 18–24 month old, c.1895. Lots of lace and frills. In pristine condition and was obviously kept for only the best occasions. $385.

Back view showing large ornate scalloped collar.

Matinee jacket of heavy peach silk,
beautiful hand lace and embroidery,
c.1900. Has never been worn. $85.

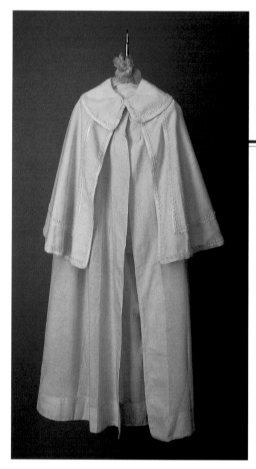

Lightweight cotton cape for chilly afternoons with silk binding, c.1880. $85.

Lovely example of ruching of the whole bodice, sleeves, and around the bottom 2 layers of this dress, c.1900. Rosebud embroidery on the left shoulder. $165.

Heavy cream silk gown with smocked yoke and a little simple embroidery, c.1930. $75.

Cape with attached collar, made of fine wool and fully lined in silk, c.1875. Superb golden tan silk embroidery. $145.

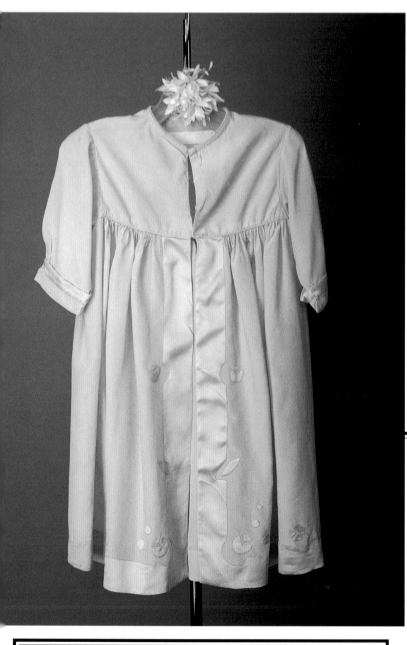

French silk and satin peach colored coat with tiny concealed buttons to the yoke, c.1920. Paris label attached inside edge of neck. $150.

Cambric cotton nightgown, c.1930. $70.

Broderie Anglaise jacket with large collar and scalloped hem to fit 6–9 month old, c.1930. $75.

Tiny baby dress to fit 4-5 month old, c.1870. Front yolk panel has been knitted in extremely fine silk with ultra fine needles. Simple, but very unusual. $150.

Baby dress with round frilled collar and long sleeves for 4–6 month old, c.1900. $75.

Short sleeved summer top with lace trim and pintucks, c.1900. Tiny buttons down the front. $75.

Batiste cotton dress with lavender embroidery to yoke, c.1920. Dropped waist with a satin ribbon threaded through. $70.

Pink corded silk coat with cotton lining and detachable lace sailor-type collar, c.1930. $70.

Organdie dress to fit 6–9 month old, c.1920. Yoke has narrow pintucks and drawn thread work. Ties at neck with 2 back button closures. $50.

Long cotton day gown with embroidered yoke on organdie material, c.1890. Organdie frill at bottom is also embroidered. Ties at the back. $185.

Long gown to fit 6–8 month old, c.1900. Made of heavy cotton, the yoke has various styles of pulled thread work with the design continued to the bottom. $175.

Cotton dress with Ayrshire work yoke, to fit 9–12 month old, c.1880. Note the 'V' of the yoke is stitched under the waistband defining the dress as being made for a girl. This dress has many horizontal pintucks to the skirt. $175.

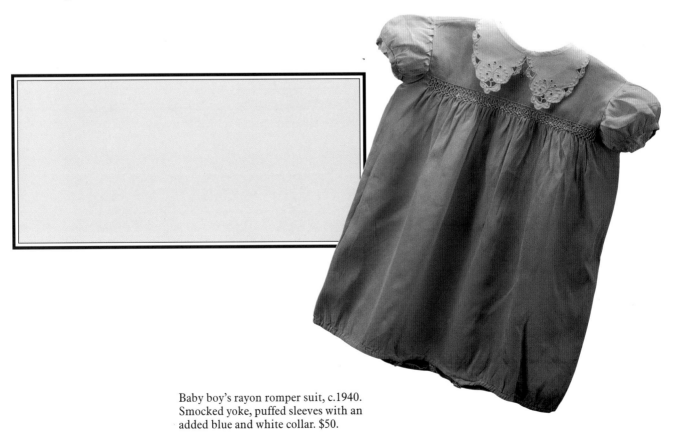

Baby boy's rayon romper suit, c.1940. Smocked yoke, puffed sleeves with an added blue and white collar. $50.

Egyptian cotton bodice with mother-of-pearl buttons to fasten front and buttons around the waist to fasten onto underpants, c.1900. $30.

Matching petticoat and pants set, c.1900. Hand embroidery and Rosepoint lace edging. Petticoat fastens on shoulders and pants button onto bodice. $65.

Eggshell blue silk dress with hand embroidered yoke, c.1950. $45.

Silk dress with pintucks and 4 rows of lace frills to the scalloped hem, c.1900. $175.

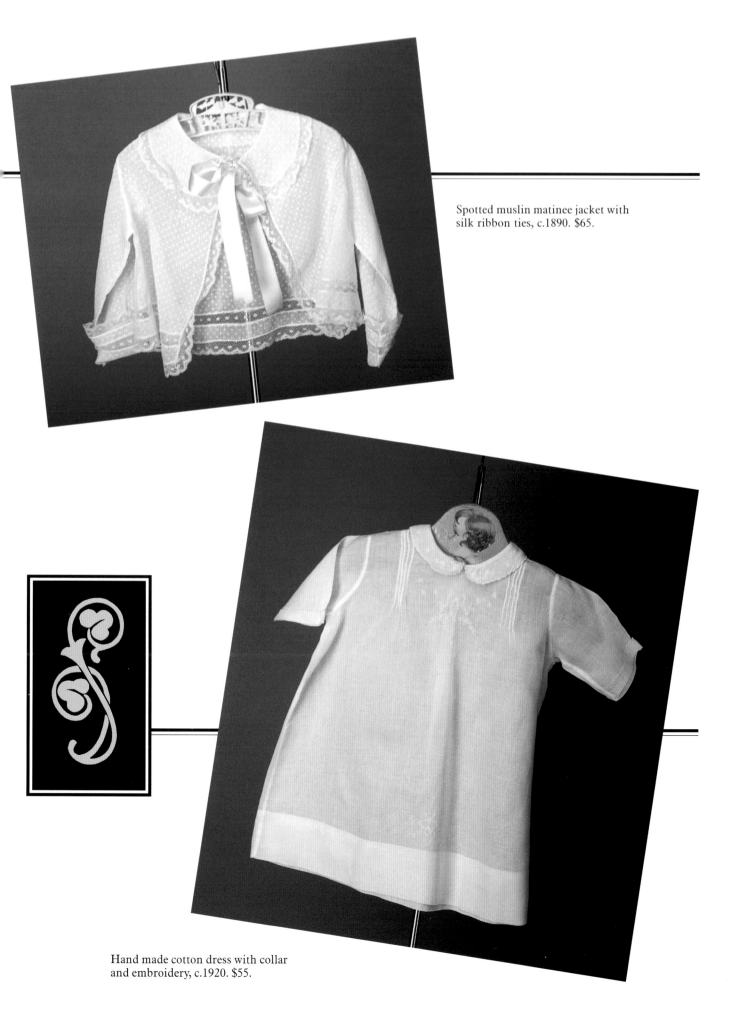

Spotted muslin matinee jacket with
silk ribbon ties, c.1890. $65.

Hand made cotton dress with collar
and embroidery, c.1920. $55.

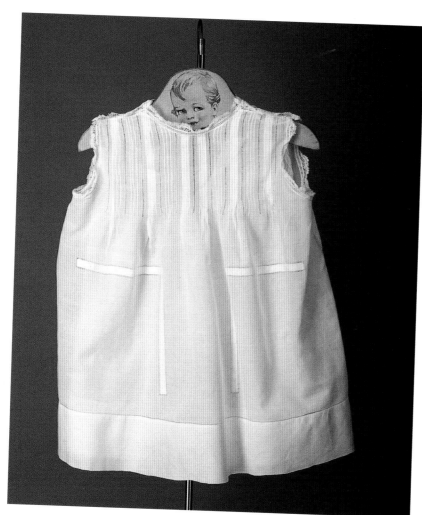

An example of one of the petticoats worn under the short dresses, c.1900. Note the hand sewing showing they were made with as much fine detail, pintucks, and lace as the gowns. $35.

Cotton under dress with ruched puffed sleeves and pintucked hem, c.1910. $50.

Fleecy lined heavy pique cotton cape for chilly days, c.1900. $85.

Cotton Broderie Anglaise trimmed cape for wearing over long gowns, c.1900. $65.

Cotton baby dress with unusual scalloped and embroidered bottom with ribbon to neck and waist. Long sleeves with turned back cuffs, c.1890. $185.

73

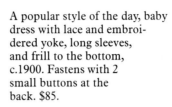

A popular style of the day, baby dress with lace and embroidered yoke, long sleeves, and frill to the bottom, c.1900. Fastens with 2 small buttons at the back. $85.

Dainty fine cotton dress with pintucks and lots of whitework embroidery all the way down the front, c.1920. Delicate lace inserts and trims. $125.

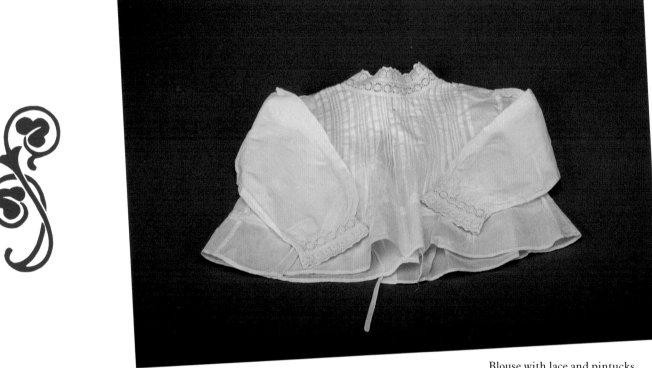

Blouse with lace and pintucks, c.1900. Buttons down the back and ties at the waist. $65.

Matching bonnet for coat.

Cream silk and silk lined coat with embroidery and matching bonnet, c.1930. $80.

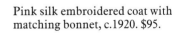

Pink silk embroidered coat with matching bonnet, c.1920. $95.

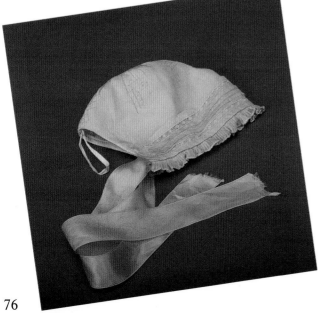

Matching bonnet for coat.

Later on, in the early 1900s, color began to appear in baby wear. Peach or pink was a favorite for girls, and blue or lemon for boys. Baby girls began to be dressed in shorter dresses by nine months and boys in romper suits—a bloused top buttoning on to baggy short pants.

In the late 1930s on until the 1950s, smocking of baby and children's clothing was popular. Many of the little dresses and boys' tops were hand smocked at the yokes.

Boy's silk suit, hand sewn with blue embroidery and smocking at the waist, c.1930. Buttons down the back and at the crotch. $80.

Silk dresses for twin girls. One has pink and green smocking, the other one blue and green. A popular style in the 1940s. $50 each.

Chapter Four

Young Girls

Early in the 19th century, very young girls were dressed like little adults, carbon copies of their mothers. They often wore white lace low necked, off the shoulder dresses with short slightly puffed sleeves. Underwear consisted of corded stays, until, when they were a little older, they graduated to wearing stiffer whalebone undergarments, covered by a camisole, long-legged lace drawers, hoops and bustles, and several petticoats. Long white or black woolen or cotton stockings and soft leather slippers or high button boots were also worn. Skirts got longer as the child became older. In the chillier weather, long sleeves were added, and capes were worn to keep out afternoon chills. Until 1885, in fact, small girls' clothing was as cumbersome and restrictive as the adult counterparts.

In the 1870s, the first mention of children's styles in fashion magazines was noted. Also, in 1870, ready-to-wear clothing became available. Around the 1860s, a sewing machine had been patented by Issac Singer that enabled clothing to be manufactured in volume.

In the 1880s, tartan and plaids became the latest fashion, and were seen at their best over the wide hoop dresses. This style was copied for children. Queen Victoria was extremely fond of plaids and tartans. Most of the Queen's furniture at Balmoral Castle in Scotland was upholstered in this design.

Good quality ribbed cotton coat with tapered sleeves and large full cape collar, would fit 3–4 year old, c.1880. The collar is extensively decorated with fine cutwork and frills and the tiniest of pearl buttons. $400.

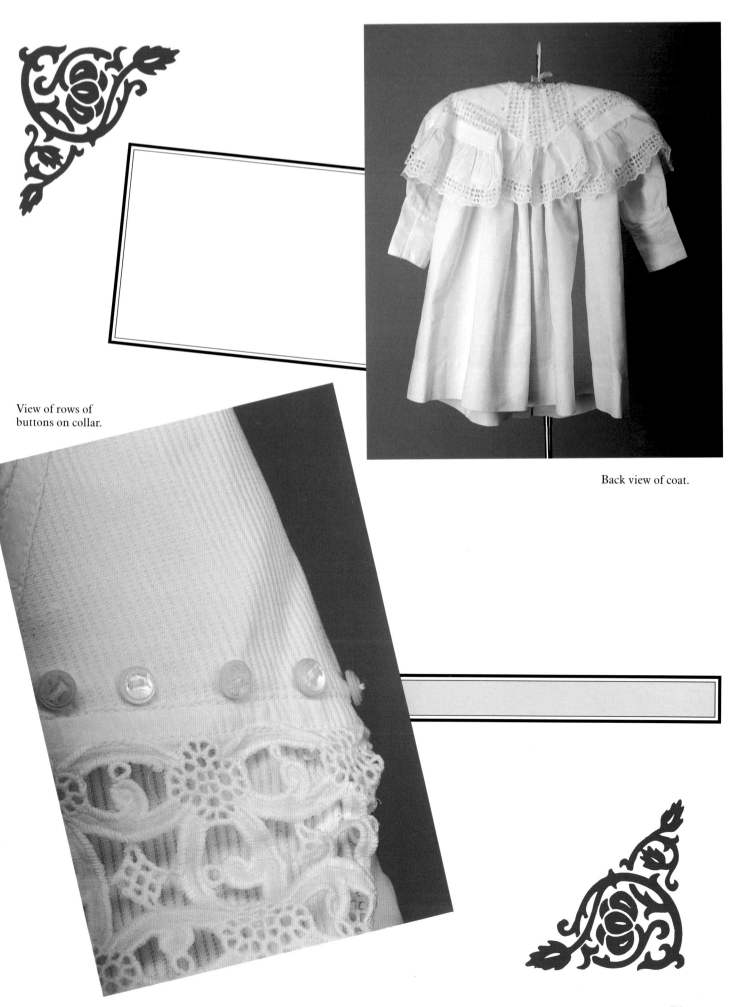

View of rows of
buttons on collar.

Back view of coat.

79

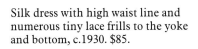
Silk dress with high waist line and numerous tiny lace frills to the yoke and bottom, c.1930. $85.

Full loose fitting embroidered cotton dress to fit 5 year old, c.1910. $95.

Beautiful long sleeved dress made in fine batiste with bobbin lace inserts and ribbon ties to the neck and cuffs, c.1870. The dress has a detachable large lace collar with 7 tiny buttons down the front. $295.

Blue floral nylon dress with stiffened buckram attached underslip, to fit 8 year old, c.1950. $55.

Floral seersucker cotton dress, all hand made with blue silk smocking and hand made buttons down the back, to fit 6–7 year old, c.1940s. $70.

Matching knickers for cotton dress.

Brown Moquette and silk trimmed coat to fit 9 year old, c.1890. The coat has a warm interlining and is lined in silk. The large collar has Guipure lace trim and buttons in the front. This coat has several narrow vertical pintucks to give it shape. $300.

Back view of coat.

Strawberry pink silk
loose dress for 2 year
old, c.1940. Tiny
pearl buttons down
front and back.
$50.

Leggings for corduroy set.

3 piece corduroy set: fleecy lined
coat, leggings, and fur trimmed
bonnet to fit 3 year old, c.1930. $165.

Leggings for blue homespun set.

Blue homespun 3 piece set: fleecy
lined coat, leggings with leather
stirrups, and bonnet, c.1940. $165.

Fine Batiste dress with unusual
embroidery and ribbon at waist,
c.1890. $245.

Girl's overdress, worn over normal clothing for play, c.1900. $75.

Pretty dress would fit 4 year old. A great deal of embroidery decorates this long sleeved gown, c.1900. $185.

Girl's underdress with pocket, c.1870.
$65.

Dotted Swiss muslin dress with blue
smocking and small collar, c.1940.
$50.

Voille dress with stand up collar, hand made with lace and frills, c.1910. $225.

Dress to fit 4 year old,
c.1880. Fine linen with Irish
crochet inserts, long sleeves
and ribbon trim. $245.

Photo of young girl taken in 1890
with white loose fitting frilled dress
and large frilled bonnet.

Girl's bloomers, c.1880. $45.

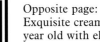

Opposite page:
Exquisite cream lace dress to fit 4 year old with elaborate embroidery and appliqué, c.1900. The dress has original pink flowered silk ribbon at the waist and down the front. $400.

White Egyptian cotton knickers with pink and blue hand embroidered flowers and elastic waist, c.1950.

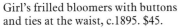

Girl's frilled bloomers with buttons and ties at the waist, c.1895. $45.

Label in the back of knickers, "Harrods" the famous London, England store.

Cotton nightshirt with puff sleeves and buttoned cuffs, c.1910. $50.

Photo taken in 1915 of little girl in white cotton dress with scalloped bottom .

Dress to fit 5–6 year old with deep frilled yoke, c.1920. $85.

Chemise with Broderie Anglaise
hem, to fit 8 year old, c.1920. $50.

White pintucked dress with fitted
waist and long sleeves, dated on the
back of the dress 1873. $225.

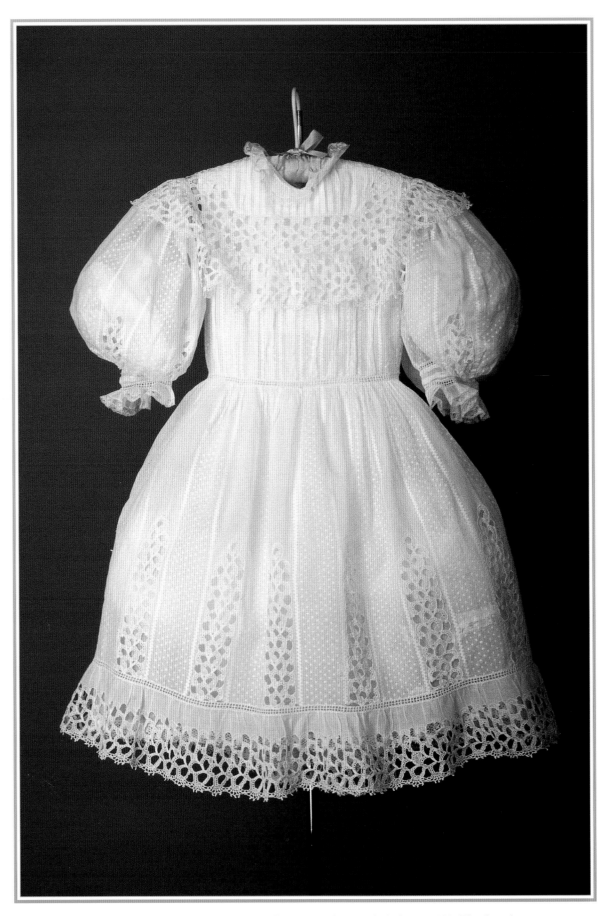

Girl's spotted muslin dress with huge puff sleeves and cutwork design, c.1880. The dress has a fitted waist and very full skirt, to fit 5–6 year old. $350.

Dress to fit 3 year old, c.1880. The bodice is all filet lace and the
bottom has both filet lace and Irish crochet lace inserts. $245.

Photo of 5-year-old girl in a silk plaid dress with a white lace collar, c.1880.

Beautiful net and lace dress with large frilled collar and bottom, with delicate embroidery and peach ribbon inserts, c.1875. $375.

96

Back view of net
and lace dress.

Photo of 2 sisters taken in 1900, one
with a plaid dress, black stockings,
and boots. The younger girl has a
white dress and similar stockings and
boots.

Photo of Victorian child in her winter ensemble.

Organdie pinafore worn to keep clothing clean. $65.

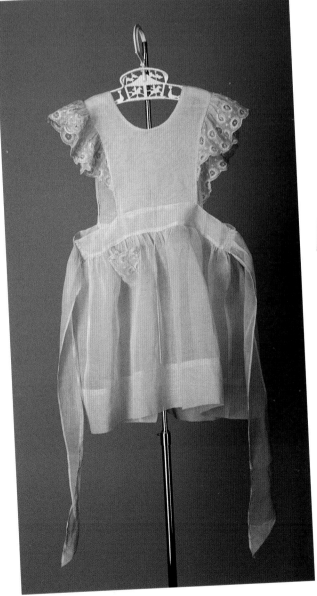

Pinafore shown as it would have been worn over a dress.

Opposite page:
Top left: Child in woolen dress and ruched bonnet, c.1880.

Bottom left: Child in long coat and bonnet, c.1895.

Top right: 4-year-old girl in sailor dress and Tam o' Shanter hat, c.1880.

Bottom right: Girl in 1940s dress with corsage.

Wm. Mills & Son,   96 & 60 Arcade, Providence.
Opp. P. O. Olneyville, R. I.

99

Dress to fit 8–9 year old, c.1890. White batiste with Valenciennes lace inserts, fitted long sleeves, and deep filled yoke . Original blue satin ribbon at the waist. $400.

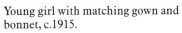

Young girl with matching gown and bonnet, c.1915.

Good quality hand made
Broderie Anglaise dress with
Peter Pan collar and
buttoned front, c.1950. $125.

A page from *Toilettes* magazine for
children, c.1900.

or Brother, Sister and Dolly...

No. 904

Little girl in hand knitted snow suit,
c.1950.

Page from *Toilettes* magazine showing the
popularity of plaids and stripes in 1909.

Spotted muslin dress with pink
smocking, c.1940. $65.

Page from children's fashion
magazine in 1900 showing beach
wear.

Photo from *Patons and Baldwins*
knitting pattern book of a 2-year-old
girl in hand knitted coat and hat,
c.1950.

Example of petticoat worn under
short dresses, c.1900.

Heavy cotton coat showing large
shawl collar with cotton lace
edging, c.1890. $285.

White pinafore worn over gown for play, c.1890. $75.

Young girl in white frilly cotton dress, c.1900.

Same pinafore worn over a dress.

Short pinafore dress, c.1930.

Photo of little girl in woolen day dress in 1920.

Pinafore dress, as shown on page 86, *top left* photo, worn over a dress.

7-year-old girl in pretty lacy dress
worn over a sweater, c.1870. Note her
wonderful shoes.

Girl and boy wearing hand knitted
dress and trousers, 1950.

Girl in sailor dress along with baby
brother in long white gown, c.1880.

Right:
4-year-old girl in
hand knitted coat
with cable pattern
down front,
c.1950.

By the late 1890s, the styles that were so disliked by the reformers were on their way out. Aesthetic and rational styles designed by Walter Crane for *'Aglaia' Journal of the Healthy and Artistic Dress Union* were in. Dresses flowed free from gathered yokes and had soft full sleeves. Girls were no longer small scale models of their mothers, and the sailor suit was as popular for girls as it was for boys.

At the tail end of the 19th century, children of both sexes were dressed in styles based on the illustrations in Kate Greenaway books.

By the 20th century, clothing was far more comfortable for children. The Art Deco period of 1920 saw waistlines dropped; skirts for girls were shorter, ending below the knee.

Dress to fit 8–9 year old with matching bonnet. This dress and bonnet belonged to the Vanderbilt family, c.1845. *Courtesy of Karen Tripp, Wings of Time Antiques.*

From 1930 onward, we see bright colors appearing in children's clothing. Silk prints, rayon, and cut velvet were popular, along with cotton and linen prints. Waistlines and full skirts returned.

In the 1940s and 1950s, little girl's dress mode was simple compared with their ancestors. A vest and perhaps a liberty bodice were worn in winter. A half slip or a full petticoat was worn under a comfortable dress, and often the pants were made to match. Long knee high stockings or short socks and leather shoes completed the simpler and less cumbersome style of dress. Hats and gloves were still considered a necessity when dressed in Sunday's best.

Chapter Five

Young Boys

Up until 1920, boys were dressed very much like the girls, until the age of five or six when they were 'breeched.'

The Victorians introduced many new styles for boys, including Russian-style box pleated tunics, Scottish kilts, Knickerbocker suits, and the ever popular and enduring sailor suit. The Prince of Wales had his portrait done in a sailor suit as early as 1846. Styles were very much influenced by the Monarch and how she dressed her children. She was especially fond of tartan kilts and sailor suits as can be seen in the various watercolors of her children. It wasn't until the late 1800s that the Little Lord Fauntleroy suit became fashionable, much to the dismay of many little boys I am sure. A generation of young boys were dressed by their mothers in fancy velvet suits with elaborate lace collars and cuffs. Long curled hair completed the picture.

Photo of 7-year-old boy in sailor suit top and knickerbockers, c.1880.

Boy's cotton coat with large cape collar and Broderie Anglaise frill, c.1880. To fit 3-year-old. $195.

Boy's coat, silk and wool mixture
with silk braid trim, to fit 4 year old,
c.1890. $155.

Dark navy blue three-piece lined
velvet knickerbocker suit: jacket
with gold buttons, pants with silk
bow trims, and a skipped cap, c.1890.
$195.

Photo taken in 1890 of a brother and sister. The boy wears a suit with an added lace collar. Similar to one in top photo.

Buttoned down large linen lace collar worn with the navy blue jacket.

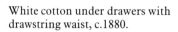

White cotton under drawers with drawstring waist, c.1880.

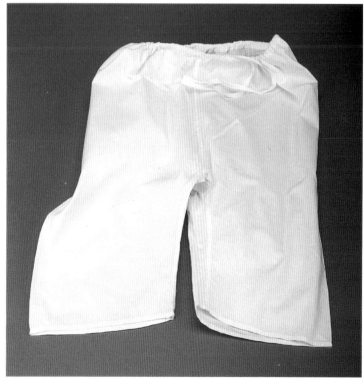

111

Boy's peach silk embroidered blouse with gold filigree buttons down the front and around the waist to fasten on to skirt, c.1850. Completely hand made.

Black velvet jacket with corded silk trim and lined striped cotton, c.1850. Skirt would have been in the same material. $245 set.

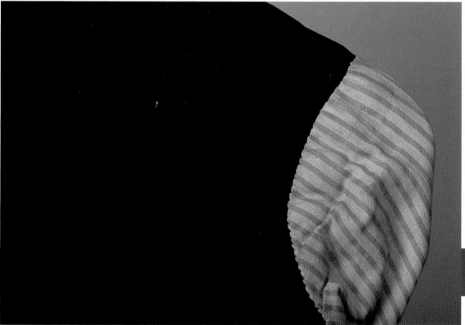

Detail showing hand stitched lining of jacket.

Family group photo of 3 little boys: the two eldest in
knickerbocker suits and the toddler in the center in a dress.
He is around 2 years old, not old enough to be 'breeched.'

Cotton Chambray nightshirt
to fit 5 year old, c.1880. $75.

2 little children dressed perhaps for a
wedding in 1900.

Photo of 3-year-old boy in 1900.

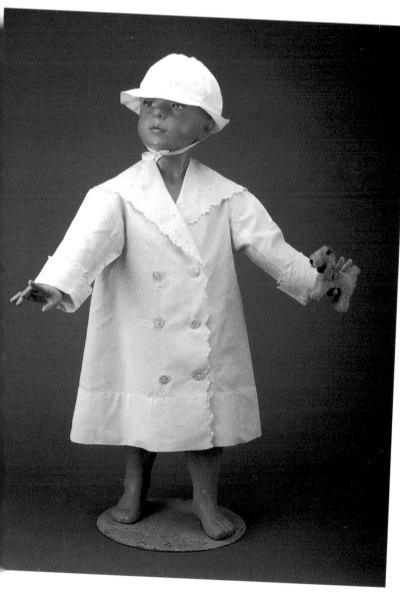

White corded cotton double breasted coat and matching hat with ties for 4-year-old boy, c.1900. $185.

Green velvet tunic top with Guipure lace trim and cotton cambric lining to go over knee length pants, c.1900. $145.

Brothers in woolen suits with knee breeches and boots, c.1910.

Photo of 4-year-old boy with striped dress and silk scarf taken in 1910.

Cotton pintucked dress with eyelet lace trim and long sleeves to fit 3-year-old boy, c.1915. $125.

Dark blue velvet blouson top with 3 large pearl buttons in front, to fit 5-year-old boy, c.1915. $65.

Picture of boy and girl taken in 1900.

3-year-old boy in 1905.

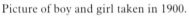

The Useful Blouse for Small Boys

Illustrations in a children's sewing catalogue of boy's fashions in 1909.

2 little boys in 1915.

7 year old in tweed knickerbocker
suit in 1920.

Two-tone velvet suit with pants
buttoning onto top at the waist,
c.1930. Lined in striped cotton. $85.

9-year-old boy in a white safari type
suit and white boots in 1920.

Cotton smocked top and linen trousers for 4 year old, c.1930. $75.

Hand made linen suit for 3 year old, with mother of pearl buttons and buckle on belt, c.1935. $75.

Small boy in 1920.

Hand embroidered silk Russian style Cossack top and pants, c.1920. $125.

Boy's fine cotton blouse with white
collar and cuffs, c.1930. $55.

Picture of twin boys taken in 1940.

Boy's fine cotton shirt with white
collar and cuffs, c.1930. $55.

Photo of family members taken in 1940.

2 piece set, c.1945: white cotton blouse and cotton pants with colorful hand embroidery. To fit 5 year old.

French jersey knit suit, c.1940. It has porcelain buttons with little hand painted tigers. Still has Paris shop pricing label attached. $125.

Children of both sexes were dressed very formally, even for play.

After the first World War (1920s), short trousers and jackets began to be worn, along with knee high socks. Knickerbocker suits had disappeared by the late 1940s, and short trouser suits prevailed. The colors were usually brown, black, gray, and navy blue. The styles for boys showed very little change from the 1930s to the 1950s.

1950 knitting pattern showing design for boy's sweaters.

Velvet jacket with silk corded braid trim, c.1870. $125.

Chapter Six

Bonnets & Bibs

Bonnets of the softest cotton and silk were a must for the newborn baby in the 19th century. The earliest bonnet seen here is the one with the Holliepoint insertion, which I spoke of earlier in Chapter Two. The matching silk bonnet and bib pictured here is exquisite and came from a baby trousseau of the Austrian Royal Family in the early 19th century. The silk is of the highest quality and the hand stitching is of the finest. This one does not appear to have even been worn and could have been a gift to the Royal baby.

Back of plain cotton bonnet with Holliepoint lace crown, c.1820.
See Christening, Chapter Two. $400.

Elaborate silk embroidered bib and bonnet, c.1850. $350.

Bonnets were not always made to match a dress, but were individually sewn. Among the lovely examples shown here are many with beautiful Ayrshire work. All of these bonnets are hand made, and some have an abundance of lace and frills. Most have three rows of fine strings around the face and also one or two at the back. These strings were pulled in when the baby was tiny and let out for the bigger child. As in everything else, the Victorians were thrifty in this field. Like the gowns, many people buy the bonnets, not only for a baby, but also for their favorite doll or merely for decoration in the home.

When a baby was dressed in a lovely day dress, a pretty bib was a natural accessory. I suspect most of the bibs that are photographed here were not very practical, but they looked nice. Some of the earlier bibs were quilted with thick cotton wadding and these would have been more functional. The bib that ties around the waist with ribbon is so decorative that it acts as a very pretty accessory added to the dress. Like the bonnets, these bibs were mostly hand made with fine stitching, and would have taken a very long time and a great deal of patience to make.

Fine ruched and frilled bonnet,
c.1880. $125.

Lace bonnet with pink silk lining
and pink silk ribbon ties, c.1910.
Unworn. $125.

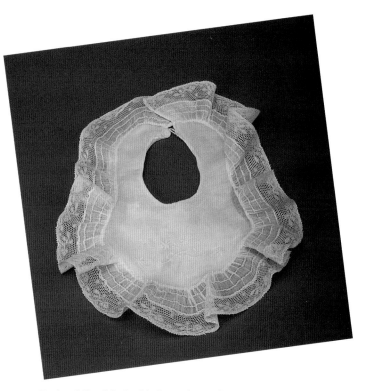

Batiste bib with double lace trim and embroidery, c.1890. $55.

Embroidered and lined bonnet with self ties, c.1890. $85.

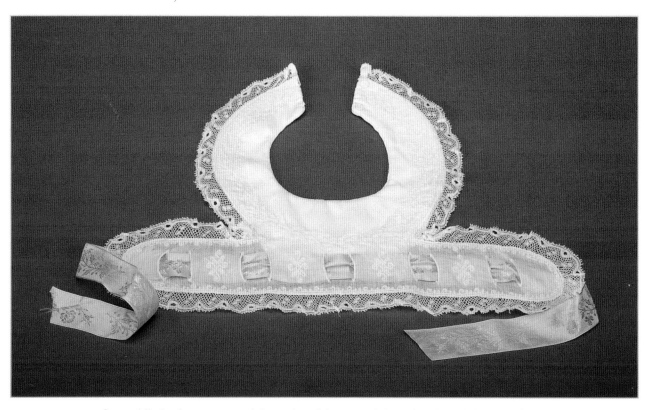

Cotton bib that buttons around the neck and ties around the waist with original blue figured silk ribbon and Buckinghamshire lace edging, c.1900. $65.

Very feminine baby bonnet made of white cotton Broderie Anglaise lace frilled in strips and around face, c.1915. $85.

Whitework bonnet with replacement ribbon, c.1880. $90.

Bonnet to fit 2 year old with lace and frills around face, c.1900. $125.

Close-up of white on white embroidery of whitework bonnet.

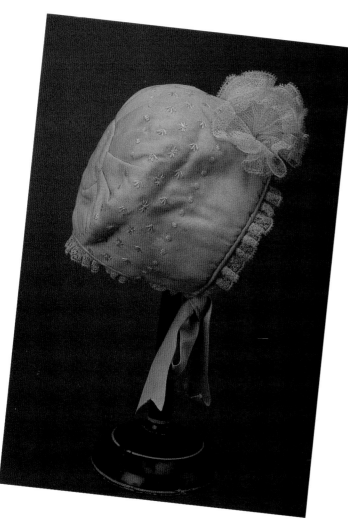

Cream silk hand embroidered bonnet
with fleecy cotton lining, c.1910. $85.

Right:
Silk cap with brocade embroidery,
c.1885. Probably worn with one of
the cream silk capes in previous
photos. $65.

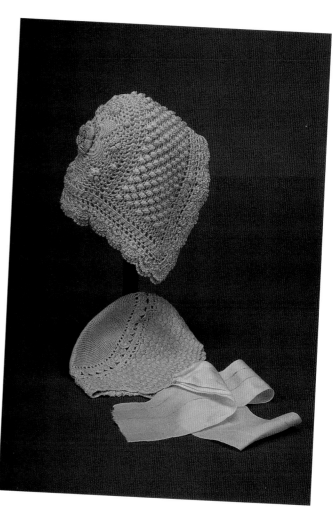

2 bonnets, c.1920. The one on the
stand is Irish crochet done in silk
thread and the other is knitted in
silk. $85 and $60.

White hand embroidered batiste
baby cap, c.1880. $85.

2 bonnets to fit little girls, c.1900. One is hand made Broderie Anglaise and the other fine cotton and lace. $75 and $95.

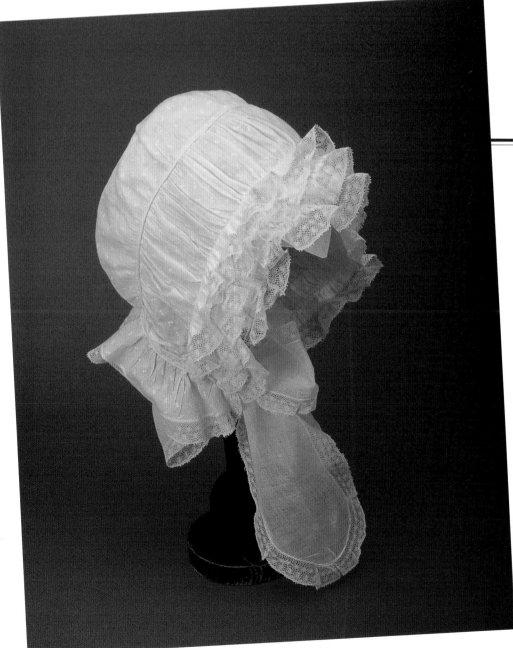

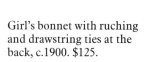

Girl's bonnet with ruching and drawstring ties at the back, c.1900. $125.

4 bibs, c.1920.
$35 each.

Toddler's white cotton bonnet with
cutwork insertions, c.1890. $125.

Fine lawn bonnet with ruched panel and
lace insertions, c.1875. 3 rows of gathered
lace frills surround the face. $95.

Child's lace fall cap,
c.1920. $75.

Silk crepe and silk lined bonnet,
probably worn with a cream silk
cape, c.1890. $75.

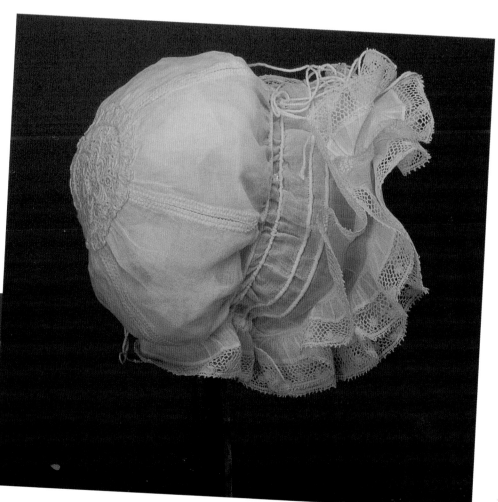

Baby bonnet with embroi-
dered crown and 4 lots of
string at the top and back
for adjusting the size,
c.1875. $95.

Bib made from the finest of cotton lawn and
trimmed with Limerick lace, c.1875. $125.

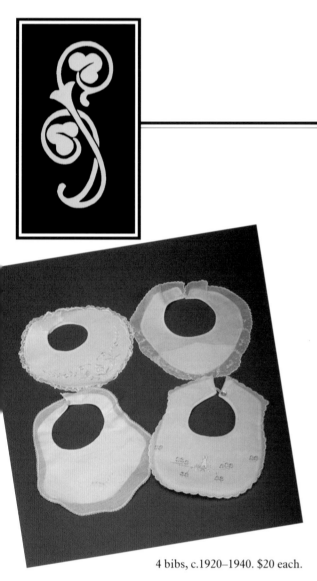

4 bibs, c.1920–1940. $20 each.

Close-up view of Ayrshire work bonnet.

2 bonnets with Ayrshire work embroidery, c.1875. $95 each.

Ayrshire work bonnet, c.1875. $100.

Back view of crown of Ayrshire work bonnet.

2 bonnets, c.1890. One has draw-strings around the face and at the neck edge and has an Ayrshire work crown. The other is Broderie Anglaise with a turned back brim. $85 each.

Crochet baby cap lined in silk with silk trims, c.1900. $65.

Batiste bonnet with all over whitework embroidery and 3 rows of ruffled Mechlin lace trim, c.1880. $125.

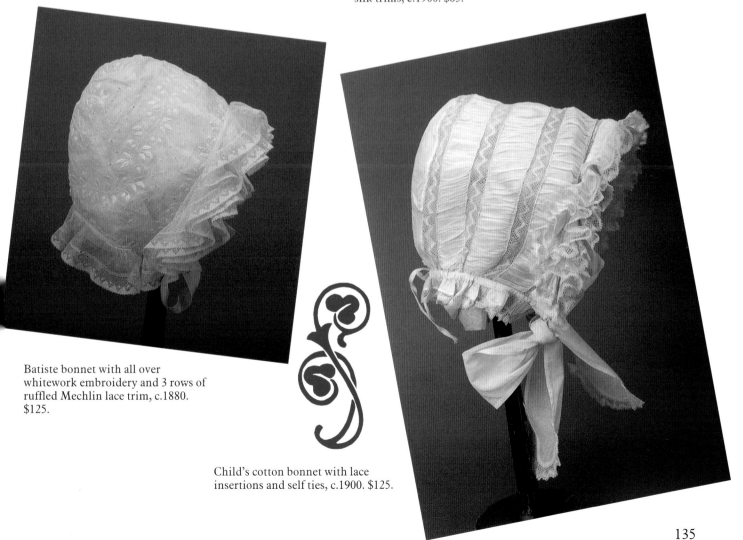

Child's cotton bonnet with lace insertions and self ties, c.1900. $125.

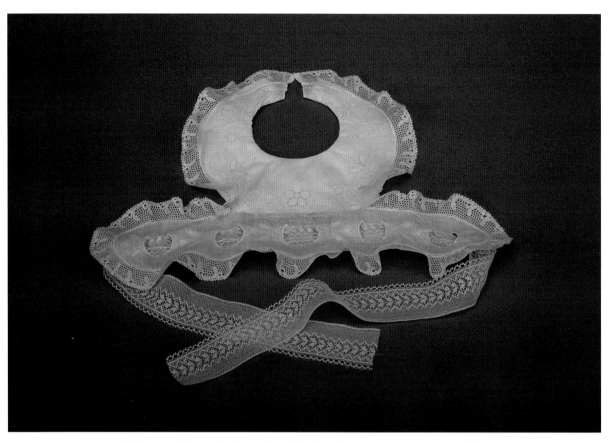

White on white embroidered baby bib that fastens around the neck with a
tiny button and ties around the waist, c.1890. $75.

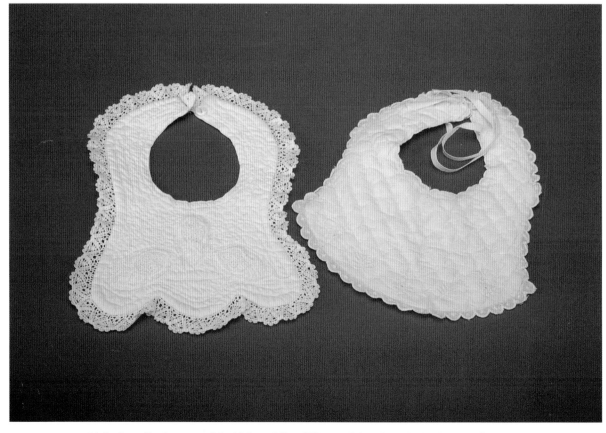

2 bibs in quilted cotton with thick wadding filling and dated on the back, 1866. $30 each.

136

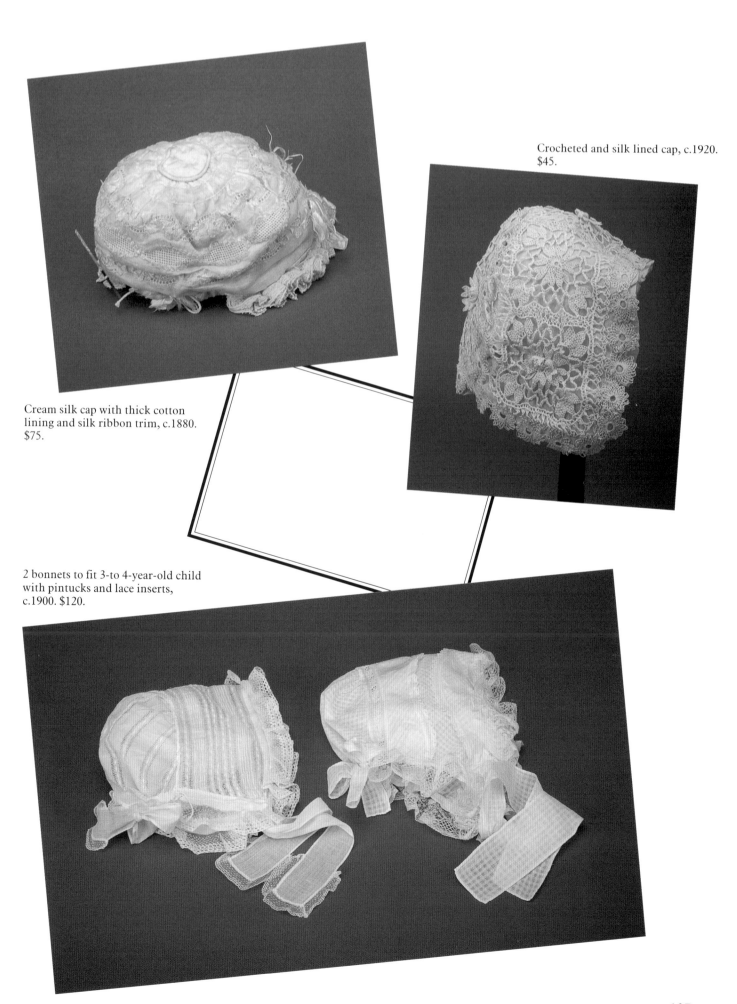

Crocheted and silk lined cap, c.1920. $45.

Cream silk cap with thick cotton lining and silk ribbon trim, c.1880. $75.

2 bonnets to fit 3-to 4-year-old child with pintucks and lace inserts, c.1900. $120.

A selection of linen bibs with counted thread work embroidery, c.1950. $15 each.

Ayrshire work bonnet with drawstrings, c.1870. $125.

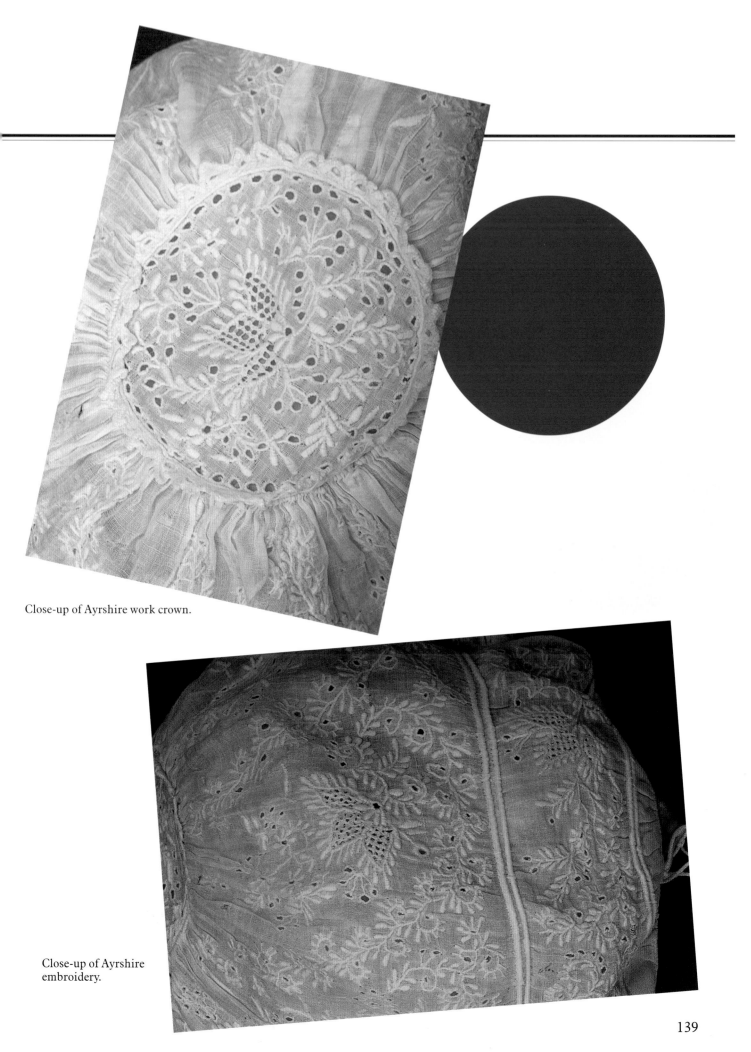

Close-up of Ayrshire work crown.

Close-up of Ayrshire
embroidery.

A crown of Ayrshire work.

Close-up of Ayrshire work crown.

Chapter Seven

Footwear

Tiny babies wore bootees for the first few months and then graduated to fine cotton socks or woolen ones for the colder months. Pure silk socks were part of a well dressed baby's wardrobe too.

The softest of kid leather was used for the toddler's first shoes.

As the child grew older, up until the 1920s, high button boots were the fashion for both boys and girls. Fine long black woolen stockings were often worn with these fashionable boots.

Two-tone button boots made from soft kid leather with a small stainless steel button hook, c.1875. $65.

Leather shoes with button strap and lighter shade of grosgrain trim, c.1890. $65.

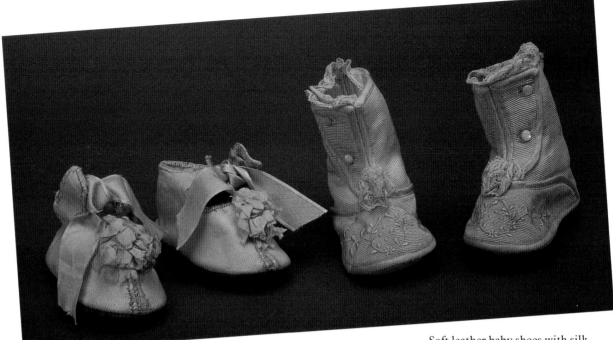

Soft leather baby shoes with silk trims and ribbed silk boots with lace and buttons, c.1900. $70 and $60.

Dutch leather shoes, c.1865. The leather is thick and the black pair have little metal fasteners in the middle, while the red ones button across the ankle. $75 a pair.

Alternate view to show the soles of the Dutch shoes. Note the heavy metal surrounds.

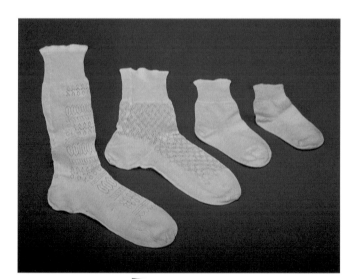

Various socks, fine knitted cotton
and pure wool, c.1900.

Button boots in soft leather, c.1890–
1900. $60.

Irish crochet shoes lined with peach
silk, c.1890. $65.

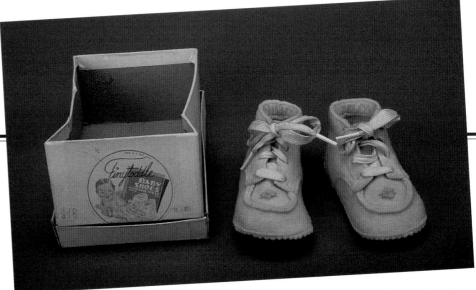

Felt boots with appliqué embroidery and their own box, c.1920. $55.

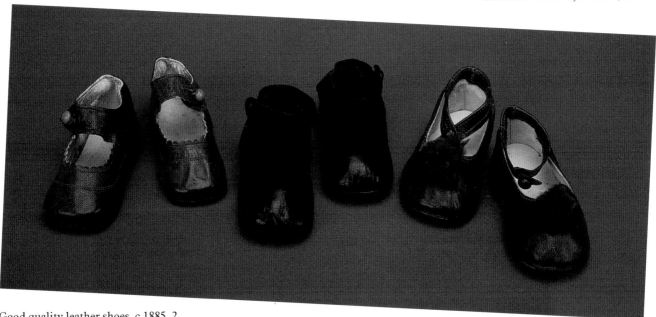

Good quality leather shoes, c.1885. 2 pairs have silk pom pom decoration. $75.

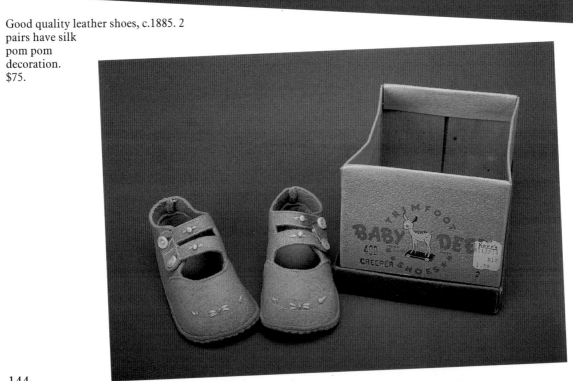

Blue felt shoes with own box, c.1920. $50.

Leather moccasins with blue silk lining, c.1920. $50.

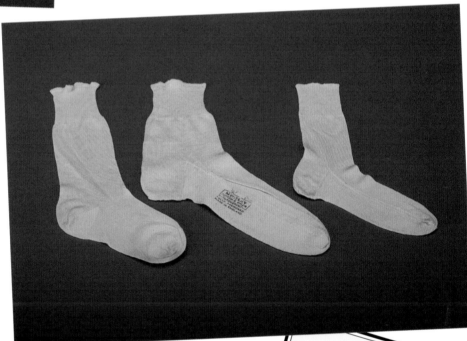

Example of various socks.

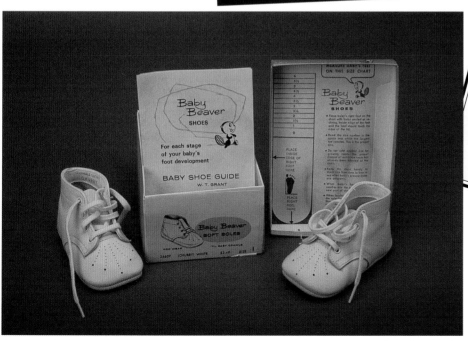

Leather boots, with box and foot sizing in the lid, c.1940. $45.

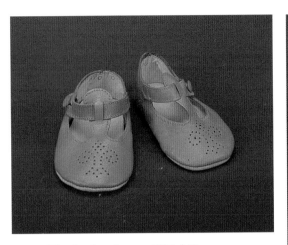

Blue leather shoes, c.1930. $40.

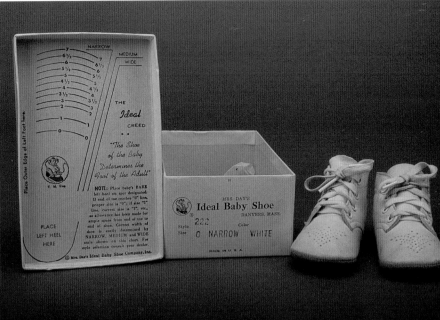

Leather boots with box, c.1950. The box has the fitting sizes in the lid. $50.

Lemon colored slippers with rabbit fur trim in their own box, c.1930. $50.

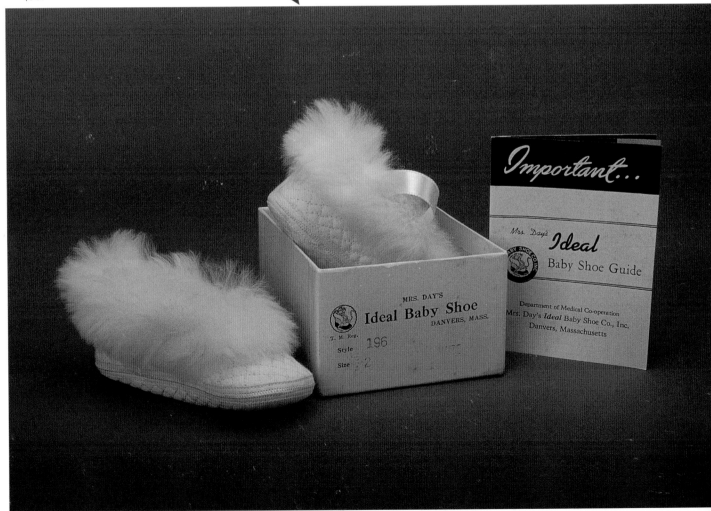

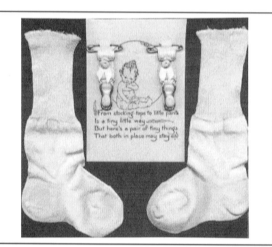

Woolen baby socks with garters, c.1920. $30.

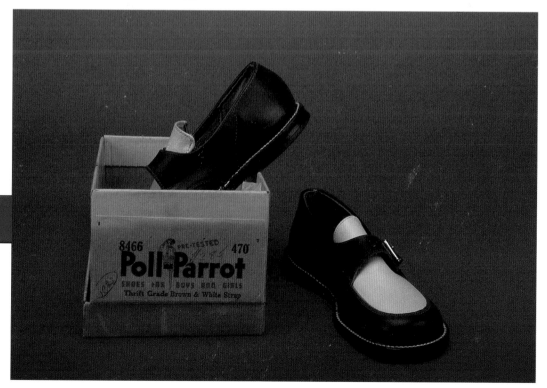

Leather two-tone sandals, c.1940. $35.

White leather boots, c.1950. $40.

Boy's leather shoes with own box, late 1950s. $40.

"Noddy" slippers, a character in Enid Blyton's books for
children, very collectible today, c.1950. $35.

Baby and children's shoes are very collectible today,
especially the earlier leather button boots.

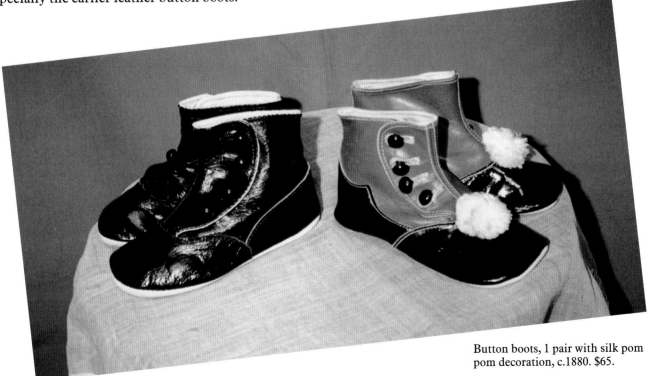

Button boots, 1 pair with silk pom
pom decoration, c.1880. $65.

Quilted slippers, 1 pair with rabbit
fur and the other with Guipure
flowers and silk ribbon, c.1910. $70.

These tiny Irish crochet slippers were probably worn with
a long white christening gown. It is a pity that such elegant
little shoes would not have been seen because of the
length of the dress.

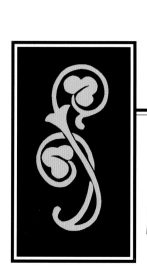

Irish crochet shoes
with ankle strap,
c.1900. $65.

Chapter Eight

Accessories

Detached lace collars, sleeves, and cuffs were part of a young child's wardrobe, to be added and removed as required.

Child's beaver fur muff with silk lining and tassels at the side with it's own box, c.1880. $125.

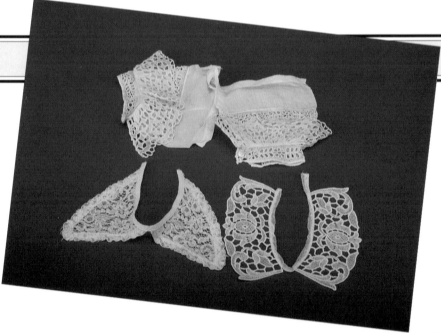

Lace collars and cuffs for adding to a plain outfit.

Girl's poke bonnet in Broderie Anglaise lace, c.1880. $125.

Various dress tops, c.1900. These were store bought to enable a person to add the skirt.

Cotton pique hat in two pieces, studs together to form the hat, c.1910. $40.

Straw bonnet with grosgrain bow, c.1915. $120.

Black velvet drawstring bag with floral silk lining, c.1900. $45.

Black velvet bonnet with silk embroidery, c.1920. $50.

Collar and yoke to add to plain clothing, c.1900.

Rabbit fur muff with warm lining and fabric doll face, c.1920. $65.

153

Lambswool muff with dog's head that has glass eyes, c.1920. $65.

Rabbit fur muff with silk lining and rubber doll face, c.1950. $45.

A Catalog of Priscilla Fancy Work Designs

THE

Fall & Winter

1916-17

Below and right:
Sewing design catalogue for
children's wear.

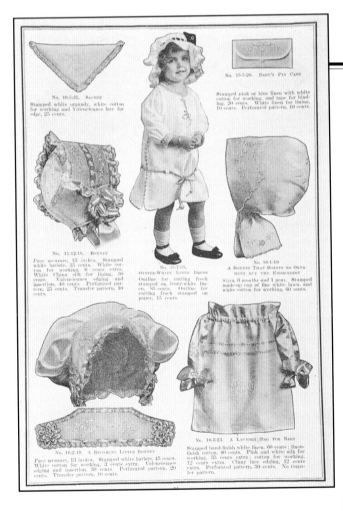

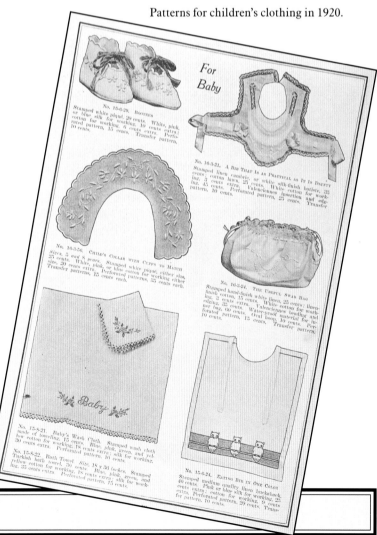

Patterns for children's clothing in 1920.

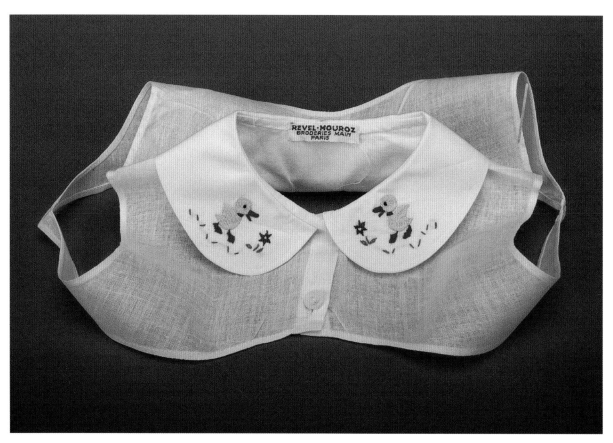

Modesty top for little boy for underneath a jacket.

Straw hat to fit 5 year old, c.1930. $45.

For girls in the winter months, warm muffs to keep small fingers cozy were almost always an accessory.

Little girls, just like their mothers, never went out without a bonnet or hat.

Silk and satin wired bonnet, c.1915. $125.

Silk bonnet with rabbit fur trim, c.1890. $145.

Straw bonnet with silk pom poms, c.1910. $125.

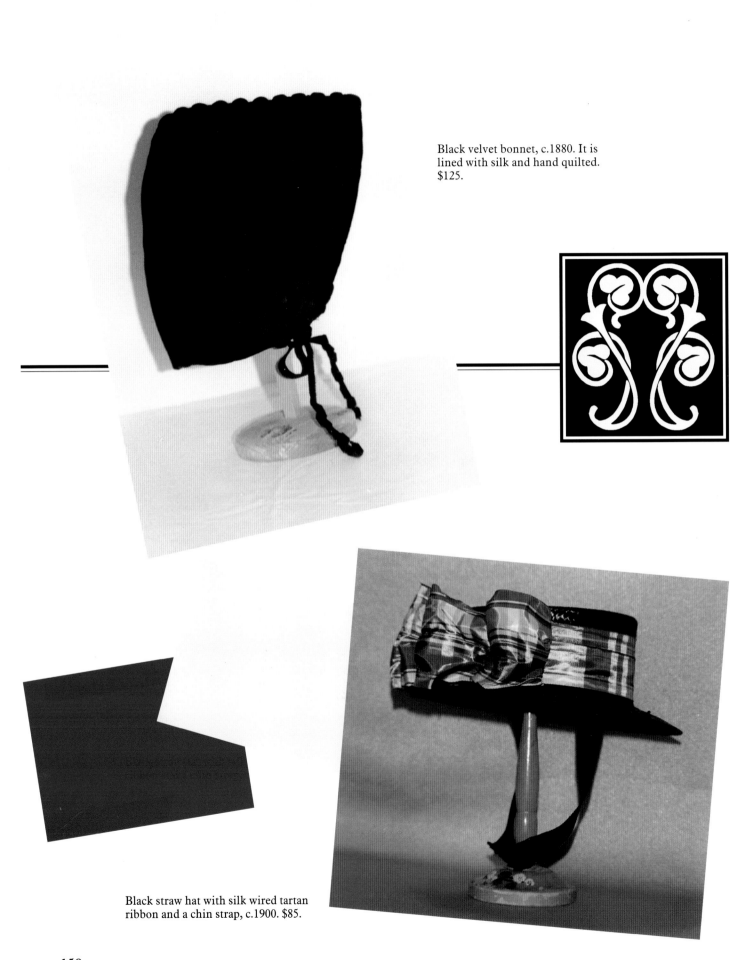

Black velvet bonnet, c.1880. It is lined with silk and hand quilted. $125.

Black straw hat with silk wired tartan ribbon and a chin strap, c.1900. $85.

Glossary

Ayrshire work: white on white embroidery with various needle worked fillings done on very fine muslin.

Baby trousseau: a baby's collection of clothing made ready for the birth.

Batiste: the finest of fine soft cotton material.

Bisque (dolls): unglazed white china that was commonly used for statuettes and dolls.

Bootees: an infant's woolen boots.

Breeched: when a young boy advanced to wearing trousers instead of dress or skirt, around the age of 5 or 6 years old.

Broderie Anglaise: strong cotton material with holes punched out in a pattern and then embroidered and oversewn.

Buckinghamshire (Bucks): English bobbin lace.

Cambric: fine cotton or linen cloth.

Camisole: lady's or child's under bodice.

Corded stays: usually stiffened cord sewn firmly with two rows of stitching onto a cotton strip to fasten tightly around the upper torso.

Cotton lawn: very fine cotton.

Darned machine net: a type of lace darned on a net background.

First shirts: fine cotton or linen garment worn next to the new born baby's skin.

Flannelette: napped (cotton fabric resembling flannel) woven wool, usually napless cloth.

Guipure: heavy almost coarse cotton with a mainly open flower design.

Holliepoint lace: early English needlepoint.

Infills: needlepoint stitching in different stitches and designs.

Layette: similar to trousseau. A collection of baby clothing and accessories made and collected in preparation for the newborn.

Limerick: Irish lace usually in a floral design and mainly used for wedding veils and collars.

Mechlin lace: Flemmish bobbin lace.

Moquette: silky crepe material.

Muslin: a soft loosely woven fine cotton.

Nunsveiling: soft fine lightweight cotton material.

Organdie: sometimes called organza; a sheer cotton fabric.

Pintucks: small sewn tucks in material usually used to shape or shorten a garment.

Pique: cotton material with raised all-over bumpy design.

Smocked/Smocking: ornamentation on cloth made by gathering it up tightly with stitches.

Valenciennes lace: Flemmish bobbin lace.

Vyella: fine smooth material, a mixture of wool and cotton.

Bibliography

Boucher, Francois. *20,000 Years of Fashion*. West, London: Thames and Hudson, 1966.

Boucher, Francois. *The History of Costume*. West, London: Thames and Hudson, 1966.

Eubank, Keith, and Tonara, Phylis. *A Survey of Historic Costume*. New York: Fairfield Publications.

Ginsburgh, Madeleine. *VICTORIAN DRESS in Photographs*. Holmes and Mrein Publishing, 1982.

Lambert, Miles. *Fashion in Photographs 1860 – 1880*. London: B.T. Batsford, 1960.

Rose, Clare. *Children's Clothes*. London: B.T. Batsford, 1989.

SECRETS!

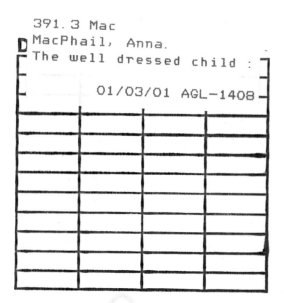